Catalan Home Cooking

Catalan Home Cooking

susaeta

Translated by:
Carole Patton

Campezo s/n – 28022 – Madrid
Tel: 913 009 100 - Fax: 913 009 118
Printed in the EU/Poland

INTRODUCTION

Extending from the Pyrenees to the lowlands of the River Ebro, from Aragón to the Mediterranean Sea, is a land which has one of the most outstanding personalities of all the territories that make up the mosaic of Hispanic peoples. During the Middle Ages, throughout the whole period of its formation, Catalonia affirmed its singularity with its constant presence on the other side of the Pyrenees.

And this communication or vicinity with France is one of the elements to be taken into account when valuing the characteristics of Catalan cuisine. But it is not the only one. Not even the most important. It is a series of geographical and historical circumstances which have contributed to forming its particular idiosyncrasy.

To begin with, we have its geographical location. Catalonia cannot be said to lie in what usually can be understood as being the North of the Iberian Peninsula. Nor can its kilometres of Mediterranean coastline confuse it with the lands that stretch to the south of the River Ebro. Situated in the north-west corner of the Mediterranean Sea, from time immemorial it was the gate of entry of diverse influences to the Iberian Peninsula. For example, during the long period of Roman dominion, the lands that today make up Catalonia participated, and sometimes very actively, in the gastronomic tastes of the time.

Ausonius, the fourth-century poet from Bordeaux, tells us how the sea of Barcelona of those days was "rich in oysters", and how –just as in other many parts of the Empire- *muria* or *garum*, (a kind of preserve that was made from fish guts, with a strong and spicy flavour, and which encouraged the drinking of numerous glasses of wine) was made in this city. This wine, probably implanted by the first Greek settlers, met at least the needs of the region.

An example of the Arab influence is maybe the liking for certain pastries based on almonds and other nuts, and the ever-present and varied abundance of spices in recipes. Different influences together with the culinary practices of peasants and the middle class and artisans of the cities resulted in the Catalan cuisine of the nineteenth century, wisely conserved and re-elaborated today by chefs in the restaurants of the Principality.

Each region of Catalonia has its own typical dishes, although the best-known ones abound in any part of the Catalan geography. Especially soups, one of the most basic of dishes and which can be found in many different ways and flavours, humble soups, easy to prepare, but which require top quality raw ingredients: thyme, mint or garlic soups. All you need is a little bread, water and, above all, olive oil. This type of oil is an essential ingredient in many Catalan dishes. But not the only one. For example, in recipes coming from inland regions, one of the most important basic ingredients is lard. Catalan salads, made with lettuce, tomato, onion and some varieties of sausages, and seasoned with oil, salt and vinegar, are so widely-accepted that it comes as no surprise to find a "Katalanische Salat" on the menus of some Central European restaurants.

As to vegetables and pulses: if you have never tasted a dish of tasty fresh, tender beans with pieces of black *butifarra* sausage, then you must not miss the chance to do so. And a similar dish can be made with peas. One of the most typical dishes, *escalivada*, is made with roasted aubergines and peppers, but can also contain potatoes, onions or tomatoes. And another, *samfaina,* made with onions, peppers, aubergines, tomatoes, garlic and, sometimes, courgettes, rather than being eaten on its own, usually accompanies all kinds of meat and poultry dishes, as well as cod.

Pork is, in fact, one of the most widely-used of meats, of which very little is wasted, since virtually all parts of the animal are put to good use: for example, pig's trotters, or the typical pork stuffings of the Ampurdán region, not forgetting the delicious pork loin with beans, *galtes de porc*, or the well-known *butifarra* sausage and beans. Pork is the main ingredient for making cold meats and sausages, an industry which has an important centre of production in Vic.

On the subject of meat, is also important to highlight the excellent beef and veal of the region of Girona. And braised lamb that is usually accompanied by the original sauce called *allioli*, made with garlic and olive oil. Sauces are also a basic ingredient of Catalan cuisine, even those made of fish, such as *suquet*, or the delicious *romesco* sauce.

Fish is also as abundant as meat. Fish soups or stews are a superb first course that, in some of their many varieties can be compared with the famous *bouillabaise* from Provence. Fish can be grilled or baked in the oven. Maybe one of the most spectacular fish dishes is *sarsuela*, a kind of mixed grill of various types of fish and shellfish.

Recipes for cod alone could fill a whole chapter. It can be prepared in *esqueixada*, which is a refreshing way to eat it raw (cured), or it can be the main ingredient for making delicious fritters, or stews such as *bacallà a la llauna*. This is a typical example of genuine Barcelona cuisine, because it was apparently the creation of certain taverns on Las Ramblas at the beginning of the 19th century, and its recipe appears in the classic treaty *La Cuynera Catalana* in1846.

Catalan desserts are abundant, varied and, some of them, an essential part of certain traditional festivities: *panellets* for Saints' Day; *turrones*, either brought from Levante or local, at Christmas*; roscón de Reyes* and San Antonio Abad*;* the *mona* - a pastry full of ingeniousness and imagination -at Easter; and the *coca* for Sant Joan [midsummer's day], to mention just a few.

Catalonia is one of the areas of Spain with the greatest wine production, with a wide range of types and qualities: *Alella,* white, dry or sweet, of a limited production and ideally drunk with fish, shellfish and desserts; *Priorat*, red, dry, strong, for meat and game dishes; *Penedès*, a white, slightly acid wine; *Ampurdán*, with excellent reds and rosés. And the region of Penedès is where the largest production of sparkling wines (*cava*) takes place in the Iberian Peninsula.

Contents

THE ANCIENT CUSTOM OF EATING A MAIN MEAL AT MIDDAY IN CATALONIA LED TO THE CREATION OF WHOLESOME HOTPOTS AND MEATY STEWS SUCH AS "ESCUDELLA I CARN D'OLLA". OTHER TYPICAL AND POPULAR STEWS AND DISHES ARE BAKED RICE CASSEROLES, FISH SOUPS OR STEWS, "ESQUEIXADES" OF COD, BROAD BEANS, HARICOT BEANS AND BUTIFARRA SAUSAGE ALONG WITH A WIDE RANGE OF SALADS, "XATÓS", "ROMESCOS", "EMPEDRATS" AND "CALÇOTS".

ARTICHOKES IN VINAIGRETTE

Serves: 4
Difficulty: Low
Required time: 60 minutes

Ingredients:

8 artichokes (same size)
500 g onions
1 dl oil
20 g flour
2 tablesp. vinegar
1 dl dry white wine
3 hard boiled eggs
1 dl stock
1 lemon
salt & pepper

Method:

- Put sliced onions into pan with a little oil. Fry over a low heat until lightly browned.
- Next add wine and allow to evaporate. Pour in stock and add vinegar.
- Clean artichokes, removing hard outer leaves, cutting tips and cleaning hearts. Rub them with lemon.
- Add whole to pan, sprinkling them with the flour. Cover and cook over a low heat for approximately 40 minutes.
- Serve in a dish accompanied by the sauce and garnished with chopped hard boiled eggs.

Artichokes in vinaigrette

Meat & liver pie, Mussara-style

Serves: 6
Difficulty: high
Required time: 3 - 4 hours

Ingredients:

Pastry:

500 g flour
2 egg yolks
1 dl oil and salt

Filling:

1 goose liver
1 kid's liver
400 g kid's meat (leg)
300 g salted mushrooms
3 apples
10 g flour
2 small glasses oil and salt
bouquet garni (thyme, rosemary, bay leaf)
salt

Method:

- Soak mushrooms for two hours to unsalt.
- Sift flour onto a workbench or board.
- Make a well in the centre and add the egg yolks and salt. Knead into a rather stiff dough.
- Make into balls, cover with a cloth and leave to rest for one hour.
- Take a shallow dish and grease base and sides with butter and a little flour to prevent the dough from sticking.
- Place rolled dough in dish ready for filling.
- Chop up liver and meat and add salt.
- Heat oil in pan and fry liver and meat gently.
- Peel and chop apples and mushrooms. Finely chop herbs (thyme, rosemary, bay leaf) and add everything to pan when meat begins to brown.
- Mix well, adding a glass of water and cook gently for more than an hour.
- Once cooked, finely mince mixture and taste for salt.
- Put mixture on pastry, and seal sides carefully with meat mixture inside.
- Bake in moderate oven for one hour.
- Serve hot or cold.

"ARRÒS A BANDA" (CATALAN FISH & POTATO RICE)

Serves: 4
Difficulty: medium
Required time: 55 minutes

Ingredients:

400 g medium grain rice
250 g angler
200 g grouper
250 g scorpion fish (or similar)
conger (or any kind of small fish)
200 g small prawns
3 onions
500 g potatoes
3 cloves of garlic
4 tomatoes
1 teasp. paprika
salt
1.5 dl olive oil
1.5 dl water

Sauce:

50 g toasted almonds
2 slices bread
saffron
2 cloves of garlic
salt & pepper

Method:

- Heat 0.5 dl of oil in a pan and fry bread, garlic, almonds. Mix in mortar together with lightly-toasted saffron and add paprika.
- In the same oil stir-fry onions and potatoes until lightly brown. Add water, sauce ingredients, cover and cook for about 20 minutes.
- When potatoes and onions are just about cooked, add fish (cleaned). Cook gently for 15 minutes, adding shrimps at the last minute.
- Heat a little oil in a paella pan, fry the garlic and grated tomatoes. Add paprika and immediately 1.5 l stock from cooking the fish (drained).
- Check seasoning.
- When boiling, add rice, distribute well. Simmer for 10 minutes or cook 8-10 minutes over a lower heat.
- Remove from heat and leave to stand a few minutes before serving.
- This dish is to be served rather dry.
- The fish, once the bones have been removed, is served with the potatoes and the onions on a separate dish accompanied by a light allioli sauce in a sauceboat.

Allioli sauce:

- Crush 3 cloves of garlic in mortar until well-crushed. Mix well with pestle, adding oil gradually, stirring all the time until the sauce thickens. Add salt.

CATALAN RICE

Serves: 6
Difficulty: medium
Required time: 50 minutes

Ingredients:

1 small, tender chicken (in portions)
chicken giblets
200 g cuttlefish (chopped)
150 g conger
200 g squid
200 g king prawns or jumbo shrimps
18 mussels
300 g tomatoes
200 g onions
1 red pepper (oven-roasted)
parsley
400 g shelled peas
600 g rice, double amount of water
oil

Sauce:

a few strands of toasted saffron
1 clove of garlic
salt
a little oil

Method:

- Singe chicken portions and clean well. Season and stir-fry in a heatproof earthenware dish. Add chopped giblets.
- Remove from dish and set to one side.
- Fry prawns and conger. Set to one side.
- In the same oil in the same dish, stir-fry the cuttlefish and squid. Cook over a gentle heat, stirring occasionally. Leave to cook for about 12 minutes.
- When the squid is browned, add finely-chopped onions. When they start to brown, add grated tomatoes and cook slowly to let the water evaporate a little.
- When cooked, add (previously-fried) chicken portions, fish and prawns.
- Stir a few times to evenly brown.
- Add (previously-cleaned) mussels and shelled peas.
- Add rice, stirring so that it does not stick to pan and fry lightly.
- Add some of the pepper cut in strips when rice is well-browned.
- Add boiling water and leave to simmer for about 18 minutes (or cook in oven).
- Just before removing from heat, add paste made in mortar with garlic, salt, toasted saffron and oil.
- When cooked, leave to stand 5 minutes before serving in same dish garnished with the rest of pepper strips.

Catalan rice

RICE WITH RABBIT

Serves: 4
Difficulty: low
Required time: 60 minutes

Ingredients:

500 g rabbit
400 g medium grain rice
3 medium-sized artichokes
250 g shelled peas
1 small onion
2 tomatoes
1 clove of garlic
1 dl oil
saffron
1.5 litres water
salt & pepper
parsley

Method:

- Clean, chop up and season rabbit.
- Heat oil in pan, fry pieces of rabbit until golden brown. Add finely-chopped onion and fry until lightly browned. Add chopped garlic and grated tomatoes and stir. Leave to cook gently.
- Meanwhile, clean artichokes, removing hard outer leaves and sprinkling with lemon juice so that they won't turn black.
- Cook artichokes in boiling salted water. When cooked, drain and set to one side.
- When rabbit mixture is ready, add boiling water. Cover pan and cook for about 30 minutes. Season.
- Check rabbit, add crushed toasted saffron, and a little pepper.
- Add peas and simmer for 10 minutes.
- Add rice, stirring it and leave to cook for 10 minutes. Add the artichokes, carefully arranging them and cook for 8-10 minutes more.
- When rice is ready, remove pan from the heat and garnish with chopped parsley. Leave to stand for a few moments and then serve.

Rice with rabbit

SARDINE & PEA OVEN-BAKED RICE

Serves: 4
Difficulty: high
Required time: 1 hour 20 minutes

Ingredients:

- *16 sardines*
- *350 g rice*
- *100 g peas*
- *1 onion*
- *3 tomatoes*
- *5 pieces of young garlic*
- *1.5 dl oil*
- *1 litre fish stock*
- *1 bay leaf*
- *saffron*
- *parsley*
- *salt*

Method:

- Wash and clean sardines carefully, removing heads. Set to one side.
- Peel and chop onion and garlic.
- In a heatproof earthenware dish, heat oil and sauté the onion. When browned, add garlic and bay leaf.
- Peel and chop tomatoes (better if very ripe) into small pieces and add to dish with a tablespoonful of water.
- Prepare fish stock in another pan by boiling 1 litre of water with the heads of the sardines.
- Add rice to sautéed tomatoes and onion and then pour the fish stock (hot) over this mixture. Add peas.
- Finely chop parsley and mix it with the saffron and a little stock from the dish. Boil for 10 minutes and then add to rice.
- Arrange sardines over rice. Season, cover dish and put into oven to finish cooking. Ensure rice is not too dry.

BAGUENY RICE (RICE WITH RABBIT & NUTS)

Serves: 4
Difficulty: high
Required time: 1 hour

Ingredients:

- *1 whole rabbit (1 kg)*
- *450 g rice*
- *700 g mushrooms*
- *2 cloves garlic*
- *4 tomatoes*
- *1 onion*
- *30 g pine nuts*
- *30 g hazelnuts*
- *1 litre water*
- *1 onion*
- *half a glass of white wine*
- *1 dl oil*
- *salt*
- *bay leaf*

Method:

- Remove liver from rabbit and set aside. Chop rest into medium-sized pieces.
- Salt rabbit pieces and liver. Heat oil in a heatproof dish and lightly fry them until golden.
- Peel the tomatoes, remove seeds and chop. Peel and chop the onion.

- Add the bay leaf and onion to pan. When the onion is brown, add tomatoes. Remove liver from pan.
- Meanwhile, wash and cook mushrooms. When tomatoes are cooked, add mushrooms to pan at the same time as the rice. Stir for a few minutes.
- Put the water in another pan along with the wine. Bring to boil and pour over the rice.
- Crush hazelnuts, pine nuts, garlic and chopped rabbit's liver in a mortar and mix well into a paste. Add to pan when boiling.
- Salt and put in oven to finish cooking for about 20 minutes.

"ARRÒS NEGRE" (CATALAN BLACK RICE)

Serves: 4
Difficulty: medium
Required time: 45 minutes

Ingredients:

400 g rice (normal grain)
500 g small cuttlefish (keep ink)
100 g onions
1 green pepper
250 g ripe tomatoes
3 cloves of garlic
2 dl oil
parsley
1.25 litre water
salt

Method:

- Clean cuttlefish, setting ink aside and chop up.
- Heat oil in a heatproof earthenware dish. Sauté cuttlefish until golden brown.
- Add finely-chopped onions and fry lightly. Then, in this order, add chopped garlic, sliced pepper and, finally, a minute later, the tomatoes. Stir well until golden brown, making sure it does not burn.
- When ready, add hot water, cover and simmer for about 20 minutes.
- Mix cuttlefish ink with a little hot water and stir into the mixture in the pan. Season.
- Increase heat and stir in rice.
- Cook uncovered over a medium heat for 18-20 minutes. Check rice is cooked through.
- Leave to stand for 5 minutes and then serve.

AUBERGINES, CADAQUÉS-STYLE

Serves: 4
Difficulty: low
Required time: 35 minutes

Ingredients:

1 kg aubergines
half a litre of oil
flour
salt

Sauce:

3 onions
500 g ripe tomatoes
1 glass dry sherry
quarter litre of vegetable stock
50 g grated cheese

Method:

- Slice the aubergines rather thickly, lightly coat in flour and fry in plenty of hot oil. Remove from pan and drain well.
- In another pan, fry the finely-chopped onion until brown.
- Add grated tomatoes and cook without covering for about 15 minutes.
- Add sherry, stock and cook for a few minutes. Add the fried aubergine slices. Check if any more stock is necessary.
- When ready, put into individual ovenproof dishes, sprinkle with grated cheese and place under grill for a few minutes until cheese has melted and is golden brown.
- Serve hot in same dish.

Aubergines, Cadaqués-style

"BULL DE ALTAFULLA" (CHICK-PEA STEW WITH MEATBALLS)

Serves: 6
Difficulty: high
Required time: 3 hours (plus time for soaking chickpeas)

Ingredients:

300 g lean minced pork
300 g minced veal (rump/shank)
300 g black butifarra sausage
300 g white butifarra sausage
3 small pig's trotters
1.3 kg chicken
500 g potatoes
300 g chick-peas
1 parsnip
1 cabbage
1 carrot
1 stick of celery
1 egg
2 cloves of garlic
20 g breadcrumbs
100 g flour
200 g pasta for soup
salt

Method:

- Soak chick-peas for 5 hours.
- Fill a large pan with 3 litres of water and add salt. Bring to the boil.
- Add pig's trotters (cut in halves lengthwise), chicken, parsnip, carrot, chopped cabbage, chick-peas and celery to pan with water.
- Mix mince well with the chopped garlic, the egg and breadcrumbs. Make mixture into a ball per person.
- After cooking for 1 hour 30 minutes, add the meatballs and butifarra. Be careful that the meatballs don't split when cooking.
- Peel and roughly-dice potatoes.
- When the meatballs are ready, remove. Add diced potatoes.
- When the potatoes are ready, remove.
- Drain stock to another pan for making soup. When boiling, add pasta to stock. Check seasoning.
- The best way to serve this stew is the following: the pasta soup as first course; the cabbage, chick-peas and potatoes as the second course, followed by the meatballs, chicken, butifarra and pig's trotters.

GRILLED BUTIFARRA SAUSAGE & BEANS

Serves: 4
Difficulty: low
Required time: 35 minutes

Ingredients:

500 g butifarra sausage (raw)
600 g beans (pre-cooked)
3 cloves of garlic
salt
oil
parsley

Method:

- Make sure the beans are cooked before starting.

- Prepare the grill (preferably a barbecue).
- Place carefully-skewed sausages under grill (or on the barbecue), ensuring it is not too hot so that the sausages will cook inside.
- Heat oil (preferably from sausages) in a pan and stir-fry beans.
- When the sausages are ready, cut each one into 4 pieces. Serve on a plate accompanied with the beans and garnished with chopped garlic and parsley.

"Calçotada de Valls" (Barbecued spring onions)

Serves: 6
Difficulty: low
Required time: 45 minutes

Ingredients:

18 calçots (young spring onions) per person

"Salbitxada" sauce:

12 ripe tomatoes
100 g roasted hazelnuts
4 cloves of garlic
1 sprig of mint
1 sprig of parsley
quarter litre of oil
vinegar
good-quality paprika
salt
black pepper
2 small slices of bread

Method:

Clean *calçots*, cutting off their roots and removing any soil.

- Barbecue/grill them, turning frequently, until brown on the outside and cooked on the inside. (Approximately 15 minutes).
- Serve accompanied by sauce. (They are typically served on a slate!)
- Calçots are eaten with the fingers. Peel off browned part until you get to the inner white part.
- Dip in sauce and eat.

Sauce:

- Roast tomatoes and onions. Peel.
- Crush garlic, hazelnuts, mint, parsley and bread (previously-soaked in vinegar).
- Add paprika and tomatoes, mixing well into a paste.
- Add oil gradually. Check seasoning. Add more pepper/salt if required.

Suggestion:

This is a delicious dish which is typically eaten in the open air during the *calçot* season.

CANNELLONI, BARCELONA-STYLE

Serves: 4
Difficulty: high
Required time: 1 hour, 15 minutes

Ingredients:

12 sheets of cannelloni
1 lamb brain
250 g pork (diced)
1 chicken breast
2 chicken livers
1 small onion
2 ripe tomatoes
1 truffle
1 glass Rancio wine
1 tablesp. flour
2 dl milk
oil
salt & pepper
20 g butter

White sauce:

0.5 litre milk
40 g butter
40 g flour
50 g grated cheese
salt & pepper
grated nutmeg

Method:

- Boil cannelloni (placing them carefully one by one) in plenty of salted boiling water. Cook for about 15 minutes, stirring occasionally.
- Once cooked, remove from pan and put into another one with cold water. A few minutes later, remove from cold water and drain carefully. Place them side by side on a clean cloth.
- Heat a little oil in a pan and sauté the pieces of meat and boned chicken breast until golden brown.
- Add the liver and finely-chopped onion, stir-frying before adding the grated tomatoes. Pour in the wine and cook for a few minutes until the wine has evaporated.
- Add the brain (cleaned) and season with salt and pepper.
- Finely mince all meats (preferably with a food processor).
- Put meat back into pan together with chopped truffle. Cook for 5 minutes.
- Remove pan from heat and allow to cool.
- Fill each cannelloni sheet with a little of this mixture and roll up, placing them one next to the other in an oven-proof dish the bottom of which is coated in white sauce*.
- Pour the rest of the sauce over the cannelloni. Sprinkle with grated cheese and place under hot grill until cheese is browned. Serve.

*White sauce:

- Melt butter in a small pan. Add the flour and cook a little, stirring all the time, gradually adding the milk and making sure that no lumps are formed (best done with a hand mixer). Cook slowly, stirring all the time. When the sauce has thickened, add salt, pepper and nutmeg.

Cannelloni, Barcelona-style

SNAILS "A LA LLOSA"

Serves: 4
Difficulty: medium
Required time: 30 minutes

Ingredients:

- *2 kg snails*
- *3 cloves of garlic*
- *half dl oil*
- *salt*
- *a little hay/straw*
- *1 sprig of olive*

Method:

- Make an *allioli* sauce by crushing garlic in a mortar with the oil. Set to one side.
- Place snails (well-cleaned) bottom up on a slab of stone and salt them. Cover with the hay/straw and olive sprig and set alight. When totally burnt, clear straw away from snails.
- Serve hot, removing snails from their shells with a small skewer and accompany with the *allioli* sauce.

SNAILS, BOADES-STYLE

Serves: 6
Difficulty: high
Required time: 1 hour 30 minutes

Ingredients:

- *3 kg snails*
- *200 g fat bacon*
- *125 g lean ham*
- *125 white butifarra sausage*
- *1 dl oil*
- *2 eggs*
- *200 g pine nuts*
- *50 g flour*
- *50 g lard*
- *2 sprigs of fresh mint*
- *salt*

Method:

- Clean snails well with salted water. Place in a pan, cover them with water and heat slowly until the snails start coming out of their shells. When this happens, remove the latter and turn heat up. Bring to the boil. Strain snails.
- Meanwhile, chop up the bacon, ham and butifarra into little pieces.
- Melt the lard in a heatproof earthenware dish and fry the bacon. When the bacon is nearly ready, add the ham and the butifarra. Cook for 2 minutes and then add the snails and the mint. Sprinkle with flour carefully so that no lumps form, adding 2 glasses of water.
- Season and mix well with a wooden spoon.
- Peel and toast the pine nuts and add to dish. Cover pan and cook over a low heat.
- About 5 minutes before thoroughly cooked, mix egg yolks with a little water and add to dish. Blend in well. Check seasoning and serve.

Snails, Boades-style

SAUSAGE & MEAT OVEN-BAKED OMELETTE

Serves: 6
Difficulty: medium
Required time: 3 hours

Ingredients:

200 g pig's dewlap and snout
200 g veal rump/shank
100 g lean pork
100 g raw longaniza sausage
100 g black butifarra sausage
600 g chicken
10 g lard
4 eggs
celery
1 onion
1 stick of cinnamon (optional)
2 cloves
salt
a little sugar

Method:

- Stick cloves into the onion.
- Half-fill a large pan with water and put in veal, snout, dewlap, chicken, pork, sausages, celery, salt, onion with cloves and cinnamon.
- Boil until the meat is tender.
- Remove meat from pan and use the stock to make soup.
- Beat the eggs.
- Grease a shallow earthenware oven dish with butter.
- Cut the meat up in equal-sized pieces and mix with the sugar and eggs, then pour mixture into earthenware dish.
- Cook in hot oven for 15 minutes until eggs are set.

ANCHOVY COCA

Serves: 6
Difficulty: medium
Required time: 45 minutes (with another 5 hours for the dough to rise)

Ingredients:

For dough:

600 g flour
15 g yeast
20 g butter
1 glass of warm water
salt

For topping:

1.200 kg anchovies
4 dl oil
5 cloves of garlic
parsley
salt & pepper

Method:

- Mix flour and yeast and sift into a heap onto a board. Make a well in the centre and add the salt, butter and warm water gradually, whilst kneading into a smooth dough.
- Cover with a cloth and leave in a warm place to rise (at least 5 hours).
- Meanwhile, wash the anchovies, drain well and season.
- When dough is risen, add half the oil and mix well in until the dough is oily.

- Grease a baking tray and spread dough out well.
- Arrange anchovies over dough and spread with a little oil.
- Bake in oven for approximately 25-30 minutes until the dough is golden brown.
- Add the finely-chopped garlic and parsley and the rest of the oil 5 minutes before the end.
- Best served hot.

MACKEREL & AUBERGINE COCA

Serves: 4
Difficulty: medium
Required time: 1 hour 10 minutes (plus rising time for dough)

Ingredients:

For dough:

500 g flour
30 g pressed yeast
salt
1 glass of warm water
30 g butter
1 dl oil

Topping.

6 ripe tomatoes
3 onions
4 mackerels
3 aubergines
3 red peppers
salt
1 dl oil

Method:

- Mix flour and yeast and sift into a heap onto a board. Make a well in the centre and add the salt, butter and warm water gradually, whilst kneading into a smooth dough.
- Cover with a cloth and leave to rise for about 3 hours.
- When dough has risen, knead again on the board, mixing in oil until firm, smooth and elastic. Cover and allow to rise again for 30 minutes.
- Meanwhile, roast the peppers and aubergines. Peel and remove seeds and cut into strips.
- Grease a baking tray and spread the dough into a circle (with oiled hands). Arrange onion (cut into rings), the chopped tomatoes, the peppers and aubergines and the clean mackerel cut into pieces. Drizzle with oil.
- Bake in preheated oven at 180°C for about 30 minutes.
- Best served hot.

PUMPKIN PASTIES

Serves: 6
Difficulty: low
Required time: 1 hour (without counting the resting time for the pumpkin)

Ingredients:

200 g pastry dough per pasty
2 kg pumpkin
200 g currants
5 cloves of garlic
2 small glasses of oil
parsley
sugar
salt & pepper

Method:

- The evening before, peel and slice the pumpkin, leaving it overnight to "sweat".
- On a well-floured board, roll out each portion of dough into thin rounds.
- Drain the pumpkin slices well with your hands and place a small heap in the centre of each round. Add a few currants, chopped garlic and parsley, salt, pepper and a little sugar if the pumpkin is not very sweet.
- Sprinkle with oil.
- Brush the edges with water and fold one half over the other, pressing the edges well together to seal.
- Place pasties on a greased baking tray and bake in a low oven for about 30 minutes.

"EMPEDRAT", AMPURDÁN-STYLE (BEANS AND CODFISH IN VINAIGRETTE)

Serves: 6
Difficulty: low
Required time: 30 minutes

Ingredients:

600 g cured codfish
800 g green tomatoes
100 g pickled pepper
250 g white beans
2 medium onions
3 boiled eggs
6 shallots
1 sprig of parsley
2.5 dl of oil
vinegar
pepper

Method:

- Cut the codfish into strips and soak for 3-4 hours to remove salt.
- Cut tomatoes into wedges and the onions into strips.
- Boil the beans and set to one side to cool.
- Drain the cod well and mix with the tomatoes, onions, oil, a few drops of vinegar and pepper to taste.
- Put in an earthenware dish together with the chopped pickled pepper, the shallots cut in four and the hard boiled eggs sliced in two.
- Sprinkle with chopped parsley and a little oil.

Pumpkin pasties

"EMPEDRAT" (BEANS AND CODFISH IN VINAIGRETTE)

Serves: 4
Difficulty: low
Required time: 1 hour 30 minutes

Ingredients:

300 g haricot beans
400 g cured codfish
2 hard boiled eggs
parsley
4 salad tomatoes
4 shallots
black and green olives
2 dl oil
salt
vinegar

Method:

- Cook the beans in warm water. (If they are good quality it won't be necessary to soak them beforehand).
- When cooked, add the salt. Remove from heat and set to one side to cool completely.
- Cut the cod into strips and soak in water or directly under the tap.
- In individual dishes, place the following layers: cooked beans, cod, tomatoes cut into wedges and chopped onion. Season with oil, vinegar and salt
- Garnish with half a boiled egg and olives. Sprinkle with a little finely chopped parsley. Serve.

"ESCALIVADA" (ROASTED VEGETABLES)

Serves: 4
Difficulty: low
Required time: 25 minutes

Ingredients:

8 red peppers
8 aubergines
2 cloves of garlic
1.5 dl oil
a little vinegar
salt

Method:

- Place the aubergines and peppers directly over the barbecue flames (or under the oven grill), turning frequently, until the outer skin is nearly burnt.
- When ready, remove from heat and wrap in a cloth. When cold, peel, remove all seeds and rinse under a cold tap.
- Cut into strips and arrange on a dish. Sprinkle with chopped garlic, vinegar, oil and salt.

Suggestion:

Tomatoes, onions and potatoes can also be grilled/roasted in the same way.

"Escalivada"

"ESCUDELLA" (MEAT & VEGETABLE STEW)

Serves: 6
Difficulty: low
Required time: 1 hour 30 minutes

Ingredients:

200 g veal (leg)
200 g fat bacon
half a chicken
1 pig's bone
1 kg calf bones
250 g potatoes
150 g carrots
100 g haricot beans
100 g cabbage
100 g onion
1 leek
150 g rice
150 g noodles
1 dl oil

Method:

- Put all the bones into a pan of water with a little salt to make stock.
- Cook the beans in another pot and set aside.
- Dice veal, chop up chicken and fry them with the bacon in a little oil.
- Dice the vegetables and add them to the pan when the meat starts going golden brown. Pour in a little of the stock and boil for 40 minutes.
- Add the rice, noodles and beans. Mix well and simmer for 15 minutes.

"ESCUDELLA I CARN D'OLLA" (CATALAN HOTPOT)

Serves: 6
Difficulty: high
Required time: 3 hours 30 minutes

Ingredients:

500 g veal
quarter hen
chicken
chicken giblets
200 g pig's ear and snout
1 dry ham bone
100 g bacon
1 veal bone
150 g white butifarra sausage
150 g black butifarra sausage
250 g chick-peas (previously soaked for 12 hours in warm water)
250 g potatoes
1 cabbage
a little turnip
1 carrot
1 parsnip
1 leek
1 stick of celery

"Pilota" (Meatball) *

150 g minced pork
150 g minced veal
100 g streaky bacon, diced
1 egg
a little bread crumb soaked in milk
1 clove of garlic
parsley
salt
ground cinnamon
pepper

a tablesp. flour

For the soup:

300 g large pasta shapes (if possible, "galets")

Method:

- Clean and wash pig's trotters, ear and snout well. Singe the hen and chicken.
- Fill a pan with 4 litres of water. Add all the meat and bring to the boil.
- Remove foam from the top as soon as the water begins to boil.
- Add chick-peas and boil for a while.
- Add the carrot, turnip, parsnip, celery and leek. Remove foam again from surface when it appears.
- Simmer for about 1 and a half hours or until the meats are tender.
- Add the cabbage, the potatoes cut into pieces, the meatball (which we will have prepared previously*) and the sausage. Cook for 30 minutes.
- Check seasoning.
- When everything is cooked, strain stock.
- Prepare a soup with the strained stock and the pasta, which we will add when the stock is boiling. Cook for 12-15 minutes.
- Serve the soup hot, followed by the vegetables arranged on a dish and the meats on another one, after having discarded the bones. Serve hot

*Method for making the meatball:

- Put the minces and the diced bacon in a bowl. Add the egg, the chopped garlic and parsley, the bread crumb soaked in milk. Season with salt and pepper and a little cinnamon. Mix well, first with a fork and then with your fingers, until consistent and make an oval-shaped ball. Coat the ball in flour and put into the soup.

SPINACH, CATALAN-STYLE

Serves: 4
Difficulty: low
Required time: 40 minutes

Ingredients:

2 kg spinach
100 g lean ham
150 g raisins
100 g pine nuts
1 clove of garlic
oil
salt & pepper

Method:

- Clean and wash the spinach well, changing the water several times, ensuring that all earth is removed.
- Boil with very little water for about 5 minutes. Drain and leave to cool. Press to remove all the water. Chop up.
- In a large frying pan heat a little oil and sauté the garlic. When golden brown, remove the garlic and add the chopped ham. Fry lightly and then add the raisins (remove stalks, if there are any).
- When the raisins are moistened, add the pine nuts and stir-fry. Before the pine nuts are browned, add the spinach.
- Stir-fry a little over a low heat, mixing well.
- Check seasoning and add pepper.
- Serve on a hot dish.

"ESQUEIXADA" (CURED CODFISH SALAD WITH VINAIGRETTE)

Serves: 4
Difficulty: low
Required time: 20 minutes (plus 3-4 hours for soaking the cod)

Ingredients:

300 g cured cod (thick part)
2 large tomatoes
3 large shallots
150 g green and black olives
1.5 dl oil
half dl vinegar
salt & pepper

Method:

- Cut the fish into strips and soak in water to desalt (3-4 hours).
- Peel and chop the onions and leave for 10-15 minutes in salted water.
- Meanwhile, prepare the vinaigrette by mixing the oil, vinegar, salt and pepper.
- Dress the tomatoes, cut in wedges, with the vinaigrette.
- Arrange the fish on a dish and cover with the onion, olives and tomatoes.

BEAN & PORK STEW

Serves: 4
Difficulty: medium
Required time: 50 minutes (plus time for soaking beans: 4 hours)

Ingredients:

550 g haricot beans
200 g fat bacon
500 g pork
1 onion
4 tomatoes
1 green pepper
1 carrot
1 dl oil
1 sprig of parsley
thyme
bay leaf
salt

Method:

- Four hours before beginning the recipe, soak beans in water and bring them to boil. Drain and set to one side.
- Peel and finely chop the onion and tomatoes. Slice the carrot. Finely chop the parsley and slice the pepper.
- Heat the oil in a pan and lightly brown the bacon and pork for a few minutes. Add the onion, carrot, parsley, thyme and bay leaf.
- When the onion is golden brown, add the tomatoes and stir-fry for about 10 minutes.
- Add the beans and the pepper.
- Cover with water and check seasoning. Simmer.
- When ready, cut the bacon and pork into medium-sized pieces. Serve hot.

BEAN & NOODLE SOUP

Serves: 4
Difficulty: medium
Required time: 3 hours (plus time for soaking beans)

Ingredients:

1 ham bone
150 g potatoes
100 g peas
150 g broad beans
150 g haricot beans
1 small cabbage
100 g noodles
15 g lard
30 g flour
salt

Method:

- Soak the haricot beans in water 3 hours before starting.
- Fill a pot with 2 litres of water and boil the ham bone for 1 hour 30 minutes.
- Dice the cabbage and potatoes and add to the ham stock along with the broad beans, peas and haricot beans. Add salt.
- Stir frequently.
- Rub the lard into the flour and make four balls (dumplings). Add the dumplings together with the noodles 10 minutes before serving.

NOODLES WITH PORK RIBS & SAUSAGE

Serves: 4
Difficulty: low
Required time: 1 hour

Ingredients:

150 g pork ribs
100 g pork sausages
400 g thick noodles
0.75 litre stock
1 onion
1 clove of garlic
250 g ripe tomatoes
oil
parsley
salt & pepper

Method:

- Fry the chopped ribs in a heatproof earthenware dish. When they start going brown, add the finely-chopped onion and garlic and sauté. Then add the grated tomatoes and cook over a low heat for about 10 minutes.
- Pour in the hot stock and cook for about 10 minutes or until the ribs are tender.
- Add the noodles and season. Cook slowly for about 12 minutes, stirring carefully. The pasta must not be too soft.
- If there is not enough stock, more can be added, but make sure it is boiling hot when poured in.
- Check seasoning. Serve in the same dish garnished with chopped parsley.

Bean & noodle soup

NOODLES WITH CUTTLEFISH & KING PRAWNS

Serves: 4
Difficulty: medium
Required time: 1 hour 30 minutes

Ingredients:

400 g thick noodles
650 g king prawns
200 g cuttlefish
100 g peas
1 onion
4 tomatoes
1 dl oil
2 small cloves of garlic
15 g almonds
2 plain biscuits
saffron
parsley
fish stock or water
salt

Method:

- Cut the cuttlefish into equal-sized pieces and fry in oil until golden.
- Add the chopped onion and sauté.
- Peel and chop the tomatoes and add to onion.
- When the tomatoes are half-cooked, add half a ladle of stock and cook for about 10-15 minutes until the stock has been absorbed.
- Cook the noodles and peas in another pan.
- Crush the garlic, almonds, parsley, saffron and biscuits in a mortar. Mix well and add a little water.
- When the stock is boiling, add the noodles and peas to the pan.
- Cook for about 10 minutes and add the mixture from the mortar.
- Add the prawns 5-7 minutes before removing the pan from the heat.

CHICK-PEAS WITH PIG'S TROTTERS & TRIPE

Serves: 4
Difficulty: high
Required time: 2 hours 25 minutes (plus time for soaking chick-peas)

Ingredients:

400 g chick-peas
4 pig's trotters
1 tripe
150 g butifarra sausage
100 g fresh fat bacon
1 carrot
1 leek
mixed herbs
200 g onion
2 tomatoes
1 bay leaf
quarter litre of stock
1 teasp. paprika
oil
salt

Method:

- Soak the chick-peas in warm water with a pinch of salt the evening before.
- When starting the recipe, drain and rinse the chick-peas.
- Fill a large pan with water and add a bay leaf. When the water starts to boil, add the chick-peas.
- Meanwhile, fill another pan with water and cook the trotters with the carrot, leek and mixed herbs. Simmer for about 2 hours.
- When the chick-peas are cooked, strain and set to one side.
- Heat the oil in a pan and sauté the chopped onion. Add the previously-diced bacon and sausage. Cook for a few minutes and add the paprika and the grated tomatoes.
- When the trotters and tripe are ready, cut the trotters in two lengthwise and cut up the tripe. Place them in the pan with the tomato mixture and stir well. Add the stock and simmer for about 10 minutes.
- Add the chick-peas and cook for a further10 minutes.
- Serve hot in the same pan.

STEWED CHICK-PEAS, CATALAN-STYLE

Serves: 4
Difficulty: medium
Required time: 2 hours 15 minutes (plus time for soaking chick-peas)

Ingredients:

600 g chick-peas
1 onion
4 ripe tomatoes
4 hard boiled eggs
oil & salt

Sauce-paste:

2 cloves of garlic
25 g roasted almonds
a few strands of saffron
parsley, pepper & salt

Method:

- Soak the chick-peas in warm water 12 hours before starting the recipe.
- Drain and rinse the soaked chick-peas and put them into a pan with boiling water, being careful the water doesn't stop boiling.
- Cover the pan and boil the chick-peas for about 2 hours.
- Heat oil in a pan and lightly fry the finely-chopped onion. When it starts going brown, add the grated tomatoes and cook for a few minutes. Add the drained cooked chick-peas, 1 ladle of the water used to boil them and simmer.
- Crush the almonds, garlic, saffron, parsley and salt. Mix well and add to chick-peas in pan. Cook for a few minutes.
- Serve garnished with hard boiled eggs cut in two.

ARTICHOKES & PEAS

Serves: 4
Difficulty: medium
Required time: 1 hour 15 minutes

Ingredients:

500 g peas
700 g artichokes
100 g fat bacon
75 g lard
1 onion
3 tomatoes
half a small glass of liquor
sprigs of mixed herbs (bay leaf, oregano, thyme, cinnamon, mint)
2 cloves
a little stock
salt & pepper

Method:

- Prepare a heatproof earthenware dish and fry the diced bacon and chopped onion.
- Peel and dice the tomatoes. Wash the shelled peas. Clean the artichokes by removing the outer leaves and cut in quarters.
- Put the vegetables into the dish. Add the herbs, cloves and liquor. Pour in stock and season.
- Cover the dish and cook for about 30 minutes.
- Remove the herbs and serve.

Stewed chick-peas, Catalan-style

BROAD BEAN & BUTIFARRA SAUSAGE STEW

Serves: 4
Difficulty: medium
Required time: 1 hour 20 minutes

Ingredients:

1.5 kg shelled broad beans
300 g fat bacon
300 g black butifarra sausage
2 onions
3 tomatoes
50 g lard
1 small glass of liquor
2 cloves of garlic
1 bay leaf
1 sprig of thyme
1 sprig of mint
pepper
meat stock or water
salt

Method:

- Heat the lard in a heatproof earthenware dish.
- Cut the fat bacon in half and fry until golden.
- Cut the onions in rings and add to the bacon together with the garlic, the mint, the thyme and bay leaf.
- When the garlic and onions are golden, add the tomatoes (peeled and chopped). Pour in the liquor and stock/water and season.
- Add the sausage (whole).
- Cover and cook slowly for about 30 minutes.
- Remove from the heat. Serve with the bacon and sausage sliced.

BROAD BEAN STEW, COLLDEJOU-STYLE

Serves: 4
Difficulty: medium
Required time: 1 hour

Ingredients:

5 kg broad beans (whole)
2 onions
3 red peppers
4 tomatoes
half kg rabbit
2 dl oil
2 tablesp. vinegar
20 g hazelnuts
4 cloves of garlic
parsley
salt

Method:

- Clean and chop rabbit and fry in oil and a little salt.
- Roast the beans, tomatoes, peppers and garlic.
- Peel the beans.
- Crush the hazelnuts, chop the parsley and mix with the roasted vegetables in a mortar.
- Cut the onions into rings and fry in a heatproof earthenware dish with the oil used for frying the rabbit.
- Add onion, rabbit and beans.
- Check seasoning and cook slowly.

Broad bean & butifarra sausage stew

"OLLA ARANESA" (MEAT, VEGETABLE & BEAN STEW)

Serves: 6
Difficulty: high
Required time: 2 hours 40 minutes

Ingredients:

8 litres water
1 ham bone
1 veal bone
half a pig's ear
half a pig's snout
200 g fresh fat bacon
quarter hen
100 g raw butifarra sausage
300 g black butifarra sausage
1 onion
2 stalks of celery
1 head of garlic
3 leeks
6 carrots
4 cloves
1 kg potatoes
half a cabbage
200 g haricot beans (cooked)
150 g noodles
50 g rice
salt & pepper

"Pilota" (meatball)*

300 g minced pork
1 egg
1 tablesp. breadcrumbs
a little flour
oil
salt & pepper

Method for soup:

- Singe the ear, snout and hen over the flame to clean. Rinse.
- Peel and dice the vegetables.
- Fill a large saucepan with the water and bring to the boil. Add the cloves, the onion, the garlic, the ear, snout, hen, bones and bacon.
- Simmer for about 45 minutes, removing foam from surface several times (to remove impurities and fat).
- Add the vegetables and simmer for a further 45 minutes, uncovered.

***Method for "pilota" (meatball):**

- Mix the minces with the egg, breadcrumbs, salt and pepper, first with a fork and then with your fingers. Work the mixture into an elongated ball, pressing it firmly. Coat it in flour and fry in the oil.
- Add the "pilota" to the stock along with the sausage.
- Cook for 30 minutes.
- Add noodles and rice
- Just before the noodles and rice are ready, add the beans (previously cooked).
- Remove the celery, garlic and bones before serving.
- Cut up the "pilota", the meats and sausage.
- Serve hot.

"Olla aranesa"

CONGER, VEGETABLE & BEAN STEW

Serves: 6
Difficulty: low
Required time: 40 minutes (having soaked and cooked the beans previously)

Ingredients:

300 g haricot beans (cooked)
300 g conger cut in 4 pieces
2 leeks
500 g potatoes
200 g Swiss chard
200 g rice
4 cloves of garlic
parsley
oil
salt

Method:

- Wash the chard and leeks carefully. Dry and cut into medium-sized pieces.
- Heat the oil in a pan and sauté the leeks. Add the chopped garlic and parsley and then the chard. Stir with a wooden spoon.
- Add the pieces of conger. When the fish is firm, stir and add approximately 2 l of water.
- Season with salt and pepper and cook for about 10 minutes.
- Meanwhile, peel, wash and dice the potatoes. Add them to the pan along with the rice. As soon as it boils, lower the heat and simmer for about 20 minutes.
- When ready, remove, drain and clean the conger pieces removing skin and bones. Cut up.
- Put back into pan and add the cooked beans.
- Serve hot in the same pan.

POTATO & COD SALAD

Serves: 4
Difficulty: low
Required time: 50 minutes (without counting the time for desalting the cod)

Ingredients:

4 tomatoes
2 onions
1.25 kg potatoes
400 g cured cod
200 g "arbequina" olives
2 red peppers
2 dl oil
salt

Method:

- Cook the potatoes whole in salted water.
- When ready, drain and slice.
- After having broken the cod into small pieces, desalt it (by soaking it in water for about 2 hours). Rinse in cold water and squeeze well in order to remove excess water.
- Slice the tomatoes, cut the onions into rings and the peppers into strips.
- Arrange in layers on a plate in the following order: potatoes, cod, tomatoes, onions, peppers and olives.
- Dress with oil and salt.
- Serve cold.

Conger, vegetable & bean stew

"ROMESCO" SAUCE

Serves: 4
Difficulty: low
Required time: 45 minutes

Ingredients:

10 ripe tomatoes
4 dried peppers
6 cloves of garlic
50 g hazelnuts
sliced bread
0.5 dl vinegar
1 dl oil
salt & pepper

Method:

- Remove seeds from the peppers before soaking in warm water for half an hour.
- Grill the tomatoes, cloves of garlic (without peeling) and sliced bread until brown.
- Crush the hazelnuts, bread, peppers and garlic and mix well into a paste. Add the tomatoes and mix.
- Slowly and gradually pour in the oil and vinegar. Season and strain.
- Serve the sauce very cold.

GARLIC SOUP

Serves: 6
Difficulty: low
Required time: 40 minutes

Ingredients:

400 g sliced bread
3 heads of garlic
1 dl oil
2.5 litres stock or water
20 g paprika
1 egg
salt

Method:

- Peel and chop garlic. Sauté in a pan with hot oil, stirring continuously until golden brown and making sure it doesn't burn.
- Drain off oil and set to one side.
- Cut the bread into thin slices and place in a dish. Add the paprika and the oil left over from frying the garlic.
- Heat the stock/water and pour into pan. Season.
- Beat the egg and add to soup.
- Serve hot.

Garlic soup

CLAM SOUP, CADAQUÉS-STYLE

Serves: 4
Difficulty: medium
Required time: 1 hour

Ingredients:

24 clams
half an onion
2 tomatoes
1 clove of garlic
1 bay leaf
30 g flour
4 slices of bread
1 hard boiled egg
oil
parsley
sweet paprika
salt

Method:

- Prepare 4 individual earthenware dishes.
- Heat the oil in a frying pan and stir-fry the chopped tomatoes, onion and garlic.
- Add the clams, flour and enough water to later fill the dishes.
- Boil for 5 minutes.
- Remove from heat and remove shells from the clams. Place the clams in the dishes.
- Strain the stock and season it with salt and pepper, then pour into the dishes.
- Put the slices of bread on top of the soup. Garnish with chopped boiled egg and parsley.
- Serve piping hot.

THYME SOUP

Serves: 4
Difficulty: low
Required time: 25 minutes

Ingredients:

4 or 5 sprigs of thyme
250 g stale bread
4 tablesp. olive oil
60 g salt
2 litres water

Method:

- Fill a pan with the water, adding the thyme and salt. Bring to the boil.
- Prepare 4 soup plates and put a fine slice of bread into each. Break a whole egg (or only the yolk) into the centre. Drizzle with oil and pour the thyme-flavoured stock (boiling) over.
- Cover with another plate for 3 minutes so that the bread will soak up the stock.
- Serve immediately.

Thyme soup

MUSSEL SOUP

Serves: 6
Difficulty: low
Required time: 45 minutes

Ingredients:

2 kg mussels
2 ripe tomatoes
2 onions
2 dl oil
sliced bread
1 litre water
a few sprigs of fennel
salt & pepper

Sauce-paste:

3 cloves of garlic
parsley
a few strands of saffron

Method:

- Clean the mussels and steam to open.
- Remove the shells and set to one side.
- Heat the oil in a pan and sauté the finely-chopped onions. Before they turn brown, add the tomatoes (peeled and chopped) and the fennel (finely-chopped).
- When cooked, add the sliced bread (not too much, as the soup must not be too thick). Stir a few times and add three quarters of the mussels, the mussel juice and the litre of water.
- Allow to boil, whisk and cook for about 30 minutes.
- Crush the garlic, parsley and saffron in a mortar. Add to the soup and turn heat up for a further 5 minutes.
- Add the rest of the whole mussels.
- Serve warm.

CHICKEN GIBLET SOUP

Serves: 4
Difficulty: low
Required time: 40 minutes

Ingredients:

300 g chicken giblets (liver, gizzard, etc.)
3 hard boiled eggs
3 cloves of garlic
4 tomatoes
2 onions
250 g toast
salt
oil

Method:

- Wash and chop giblets.
- Heat the oil in a pan and lightly fry the giblets. Add the finely-chopped onions, garlic and tomatoes and sauté until lightly golden. Add 1 and a quarter litres of water. Simmer gently.
- When the giblets are cooked, add the toast. Season.
- A few minutes later, whisk the mixture until the bread is well dissolved.
- Before serving, add the chopped hard boiled eggs.
- Serve hot.

GOOSE SOUP

Serves: 6
Difficulty: low
Required time: 1 hour 30 minutes

Ingredients:

- *1 goose breast*
- *1 goose neck*
- *1 goose gizzard*
- *1 ham bone*
- *2 leeks*
- *1 stalk of celery*
- *2 onions*
- *2 carrots*
- *2 potatoes*
- *2 parsnips*
- *300 g mushrooms*
- *3 litres water*

Method:

- Prepare stock by boiling the goose breast, neck, gizzard and the ham bone. Remove foam from surface.
- Add the celery, 1 carrot, 1 parsnip, 1 potato, 1 onion (all chopped), cover and simmer for 1 hour and 30 minutes.
- Finely chop the rest of the vegetables and sauté them in a little oil along with the mushrooms.
- When the stock is ready, remove and dice the breast. Add the breast pieces to the vegetables. After frying lightly, add the strained stock and cook for 5 minutes.
- Serve either individually in soup dishes or in a soup tureen.

ANGLER SOUP

Serves: 6
Difficulty: medium
Required time: 1 hour 15 minutes

Ingredients:

1 kg angler head and bones
150 g onion
200 g ripe tomatoes
1 sprig toasted fennel
bouquet garni (bay leaf, thyme, parsley)
salt & pepper
2 dl oil
finely sliced bread

3 cloves of garlic
25 roasted almonds
saffron

Method:

- Sauté the sliced onion in oil until golden brown. Add the tomatoes (chopped).
- Allow the liquid to evaporate.
- Meanwhile, prepare stock by boiling 2.5 litres of water with the angler head and bones, the herbs and the fennel.
- Simmer for about 30 minutes.
- Every now and again, remove the foam from the surface.
- When the stock is ready, strain and set aside any fish that there may be from the head.
- Pour the stock over the tomatoes and onion. Add the slices of bread and simmer for 15 minutes.
- Blend the bread well into the soup by whisking.
- Crush the garlic, almonds and saffron in a mortar. Mix well. Add it to the stock along with any pieces of fish.
- Simmer for about 5 minutes.
- Check seasoning.
- Serve hot.

Suggestion:

Can be garnished with steam-cooked mussels.

Angler soup

STUFFED TOMATOES, MONT ROIG-STYLE

Serves: 6
Difficulty: low
Required time: 45 minutes

Ingredients:

24 medium-sized tomatoes
800 g lean pork
2 onions
25 g flour
50 g lard
50 g breadcrumbs
2 small glasses of milk
0.5 dl oil
salt & pepper

Method:

- Melt the lard in a pan. Dice and add the meat. Season with salt and pepper.
- Once the meat has soaked up the fat, add the finely-chopped onions. Cover and cook for a few minutes, making sure the meat doesn't burn.
- Add the flour and the milk carefully to the meat, stirring well.
- When the meat is cooked, make a purée or mince. Check seasoning.
- Scald the tomatoes so they will be easier to peel.
- With a small spoon, scoop out the tomato pulp. Fill with the meat mixture (puréed or minced).
- Arrange the tomatoes in an ovenproof dish and drizzle with oil. Place in a hot oven for 3 minutes.
- Serve immediately.

FLOUR OMELETTE

Serves: 6
Difficulty: low
Required time: 35 minutes

Ingredients:

8 eggs
4 tablesp. flour
1 glass of milk
olive oil
salt & pepper

Method:

- Beat the eggs in a bowl. Add the milk. Add the flour gradually, beating carefully until the mixture is smooth and without any lumps.
- Season and set to one side for 20 minutes.
- Heat a little oil in a non-stick frying pan. Add the omelette mixture when the oil is very hot. Stir carefully with a wooden spoon. When the eggs are set on one side, turn the omelette over and cook the other side.
- Serve hot accompanied by a green salad.

Flour omelette

SAUSAGE & BEAN OMELETTE

Serves: 4
Difficulty: medium
Required time: 40 minutes

Ingredients:

Omelette:

4 eggs
100 g fat bacon
100 g white egg butifarra sausage
150 g cooked beans
oil

Sauce:

1 onion
1 tomato
20 g flour
1 clove of garlic
1 dl white wine
1 tablesp. paprika
4 dl stock
100 g white butifarra sausage
parsley
oil
pepper & salt

Sauce-paste:

6 roasted almonds
6 roasted hazelnuts
1 clove of garlic
saffron

Method:

- Heat a little oil in a non-stick frying pan. Lightly fry the diced bacon. When golden, add the beans. Stir and cook for a few minutes. Add the egg butifarra cut into slices and stir-fry a little.
- Meanwhile, heat a little oil in a pan to prepare the sauce. Add the finely-chopped onion and fry until it starts going brown. Add the chopped garlic and parsley. Pour in the wine and allow the wine to evaporate.
- Scald, peel and chop the tomatoes. Add them to the sauce. Stir in a little flour. Pour in the stock. Add the tablespoon of paprika. Stir well.
- Cover and cook for 15 minutes.
- Crush the almonds and hazelnuts in the mortar to form a paste. Add the garlic and saffron. Mix well and blend with a little stock. Add to the sauce.
- Put the omelette (previously made) in an earthenware dish. Pour sauce over and top with slices of white butifarra. Cook for 10 minutes.
- Serve in the same dish garnished with chopped parsley.

"TRINXAT DE LA CERDANYA" (BUBBLE 'N' SQUEAK)

Serves: 4
Difficulty: low
Required time: 1 hour

Ingredients:

1 cabbage
1 kg potatoes
4 pieces of streaky bacon
2 cloves of garlic
oil and salt
lard

Method:

- Fill a pan with water. When the water starts boiling, add a pinch of salt and the cabbage (washed and chopped).
- Peel the potatoes and add them to the pan. Cook for about 25 minutes. Drain well.
- Put the potatoes and cabbage into a pan. Mash and mix them well.
- Heat a little oil in a frying pan and fry the garlic (peeled). When golden, remove from the heat.
- Add the bacon and fry until golden. Set to one side.
- Add a little of this oil to the pan containing the potatoes and cabbage. Stir well.
- Put the mixture of potatoes and cabbage into the pan with the rest of the oil in which the bacon was fried. Press well and shape into an omelette. Brown well on both sides.
- When ready, garnish with the fried bacon.
- Serve immediately.

STEWED VEGETABLES & MEAT

Serves: 4
Difficulty: medium
Required time: 60 minutes

Ingredients:

2 carrots
2 leeks
4 stalks of celery
half a cabbage
half an onion
2 cloves of garlic
2 potatoes
half a parsnip
half a chicken
half a white butifarra sausage
half a black butifarra sausage
1 fresh shoulder of ham
1 veal bone
a handful of rice
a handful of thick noodles
oil
water
salt

Method:

- Peel, wash and dice vegetables finely.
- Heat the oil in a deep pan and sauté the vegetables.
- Before the vegetables are brown, add the ham and calf bones and the chopped chicken. Fry a little and then cover with water.
- Cover and simmer for about 30 minutes.
- Add the butifarra sausages, the noodles and rice. Cover again and cook for a further 15 minutes.
- Check seasoning.
- Remove the bones.
- Serve with the chicken meat separated from the bones and the sausages cut in four, 1 per serving.

"XATÓ DE SITGES" (COD, TUNA FISH AND ESCAROLE SALAD)

Serves: 4
Difficulty: low
Required time: 1 hour (plus time for soaking the peppers and fish)

Ingredients:

1 large escarole
100 g boneless cured cod
100 g cured tuna fish
4 salted anchovies
150 g "arbequína" olives
2 red tomatoes

Sauce:

2 dried red peppers
2 cloves of garlic
10 roasted almonds
2 ripe tomatoes
1 tablesp. paprika
salt
1.5 dl olive oil
4 tablesp. vinegar
chilli

Method for salad:

- Deseed and soak the peppers -without seeds- in cold water for about 2 hours.
- Tear the cod and tuna fish into small pieces and soak in cold water to desalt.
- Remove bones from anchovies and fillet them. Rinse a little to desalt.
- Wash and chop the escarole.
- Put the escarole in a large bowl. Add the tomatoes cut in wedges, the olives, the cod and tuna well drained. Garnish with the anchovy fillets.
- Dress with the sauce*.
- Serve chilled.

Method for *sauce:

- Fire-roast ("escalivar") or grill the garlic and tomatoes. Peel.
- Crush the almonds in a mortar. Add and crush the garlic and tomatoes, then the chilli, vinegar and paprika. Mix well to blend.
- Take pulp out of the dried peppers and add to the sauce. Add a little oil. Check seasoning.

Xató de Sitges

Catalunya has an infinite number of fish specialities due to its extensive coastline and ancient seafaring tradition. The fishermen of these shores have created a wide variety of succulent dishes: "l'all cremat", "suquets", "romescos", stews of squid and cod, braised fish, "sarsuelas", "frittatas" and "calderetes" of shellfish. The main thing is for the seafood to be fresh, to get its cooking point just perfect, and to dish it up accompanied by the right sauce.

FRIED EEL WITH ALMOND SAUCE

Serves: 4
Difficulty: medium
Required time: 40 minutes

Ingredients:

- *800 g eel*
- *100 g flour*
- *2.5 dl oil*
- *3 cloves of garlic*
- *1 slice of bread*
- *70 g roasted almonds*
- *parsley*
- *salt & pepper*

Method:

- Wash eel well, chop and salt. Coat lightly in flour. Heat oil in a frying pan and fry eel pieces until golden. Place fried pieces in an earthenware dish, cover with water and cook over a low heat.
- In the same frying pan and oil, fry the bread, 2 cloves of garlic and parsley. Once brown, put in a mortar along with the other clove of garlic, the skinned almonds and a little oil from the pan. Crush and mix well.
- Pour this sauce over the eels when the water reaches boiling point.
- When the eels are ready, remove pan from heat and season.

EEL WITH BEANS

Serves: 4
Difficulty: low
Required time: 40 minutes (plus soaking time)

Ingredients:

- *800 g eel*
- *400 g haricot beans*
- *4 tomatoes*
- *1 large onion*
- *3 cloves of garlic*
- *2 dl oil and salt*
- *15 g roasted hazelnuts*
- *40 g flour*
- *half a glass of white wine*
- *1 bay leaf*
- *parsley*
- *ground cinnamon & saffron*

Method:

- The evening before, soak the beans and eel in water.
- Slice the eel. Coat slices in flour and fry in hot oil. Set to one side
- In another pan, boil the beans. Drain and keep a little of their cooking water.
- Peel and chop the onions and tomatoes and fry with the bay leaf. When cooked, add the wine and let it evaporate.
- Put the eel pieces into an earthenware dish along with a little of the bean stock. Cook over a low heat.
- Crush 1 or 2 strands of saffron, the garlic, hazelnuts and parsley in a mortar. Mix with a little stock and add to the eel together with the beans. Season and cook for 10-15 minutes. Add the cinnamon 2 minutes before removing dish from heat.
- Serve in the same dish piping hot.

Eel with beans

COD, CATALAN-STYLE

Serves: 4
Difficulty: high
Required time: 1 hour 20 minutes (plus soaking time for cod)

Ingredients:

600 g cured cod
400 g potatoes
150 g peas
3 artichokes
2 hard boiled eggs
150 g flour
1 onion
3 tomatoes
3 cloves of garlic
2 dl oil
half a glass of white wine
1 bay leaf
parsley
saffron
salt & pepper

Method:

- Clean, slice and desalt cod a few hours before. Coat in flour after draining well.
- Cut the artichokes into quarters and fry lightly in oil.
- Remove the artichokes. In the same oil, fry the pieces of cod. Put everything (including the oil) in a heatproof earthenware dish and cook over a low heat.
- Peel and chop the onions and tomatoes and add to dish along with the bay leaf and wine. Once the wine has evaporated, add a little water. Cook for 10 minutes.
- Meanwhile, peel and cut potatoes into rounds and boil them in another pan along with the peas. Add the hard boiled eggs. Drain and set aside.
- Take the sauce out of the pan and strain it. Add the potatoes, artichokes and peas and pour the sauce over.
- Chop the garlic, saffron and parsley. Slice the eggs in half. 3 minutes before removing dish from heat, add eggs and mixture of chopped garlic.

COD "A LA LLAUNA"

Serves: 4
Difficulty: low
Required time: 40 minutes (plus time for soaking cod)

Ingredients:

600 g cured cod (thick part)
4 cloves of garlic
1 glass of white wine
15 g paprika
flour
2 dl olive oil
parsley
salt & pepper

Method:

- Cut the cod into medium-sized pieces and soak in water for 24 hours, changing the water 3-4 times.
- When the cod is sufficiently desalted, drain and dab dry with a cloth. Lightly coat in flour.
- Heat the oil in a frying pan.
- Fry the pieces of cod until golden and place on a metal baking tray ("llauna").
- Using the same oil, fry the garlic (peeled and finely-chopped).

- When the garlic starts to turn brown, remove pan from heat. Add the paprika and stir quickly.
- Mix in the wine and briefly return pan to the heat.
- Pour mixture over the cod.
- Sprinkle with chopped parsley and put into a hot oven for a few minutes.
- Serve on the same "llauna".

HONEY-FRIED COD

Serves: 4
Difficulty: medium
Required time: 35 minutes (plus time for soaking cod)

Ingredients:

800 g cured cod (thick part)
0.5 litre oil
200 g flour
stick of cinnamon
2 cups (coffee cups) of honey
1 bay leaf
quarter litre of water
parsley
salt

Method:

- Place the whole piece of cod in a pan, the part with skin facing upwards, covered with water. Add the bay leaf, cinnamon and parsley.
- Cook very slowly (don't boil) for a few minutes until a white foam appears on the surface.
- Remove the cod and drain it well on a cloth. Leave to cool.
- Cut cod into strips of approximately 1 cm.
- Mix nearly all the flour with the water and honey, blending well into a smooth batter (neither too runny nor too thick) for coating the cod.
- Coat the cod pieces first in the remaining flour and then in the batter.
- Heat oil in a frying pan (not too hot) and fry fish.
- Serve immediately.

COD WITH RAISINS & PINE NUTS

Serves: 4
Difficulty: medium
Required time: 60 minutes (plus 24 hours for soaking cod)

Ingredients:

700 g cured cod (thick part)
flour

For sauce:

2 dl oil
1 medium-sized onion
2 cloves of garlic
4 anchovies
50 g pine nuts
50 g raisins
1 glass of white wine
0.5 litre milk
50 g butter
parsley
salt & pepper

Method:

- Previously soak the cod in water for 24 hours, changing the water at least 3 times.
- When the cod is sufficiently desalted, drain and dab dry with a cloth.
- Coat in flour and place in an oven dish.
- In a frying pan, sauté the chopped onion and garlic.
- Wash the anchovies and carefully remove any bones. Mash the anchovies.
- Add the finely chopped parsley to the anchovies. Mix well and add to the onion and garlic.
- Pour in the wine. Allow to evaporate. Add milk and butter. Cook for a few minutes.
- Pour this sauce over the cod in the dish. Sprinkle with the pine nuts and raisins. Shake the dish a little and place in a heated oven until the sauce has been slightly absorbed.
- Serve in the same dish.

Cod with raisins & pine nuts

COD WITH TOMATO & DRIED FRUITS

Serves: 4
Difficulty: medium
Required time: 45 minutes (plus time for soaking cod)

Ingredients:

- *8 pieces cured cod, weighing 120 g each*
- *100 g pine nuts*
- *50 g raisins*
- *16 prunes*
- *4 ripe tomatoes*
- *2 shallots*
- *2 leeks*
- *2 cloves of garlic*
- *1 small glass of white wine*
- *quarter litre of olive oil*
- *flour*
- *parsley*
- *salt & pepper*

Method:

- Previously soak the cod for 24 hours, changing the water at least 3 times.
- After having dried the desalted cod well with a cloth, coat it in flour.
- Heat oil in a pan and fry the cod. Remove from pan and set aside.
- Peel and finely chop the onions and leeks. Sauté them in the same oil used for frying the cod.
- When golden, add the chopped garlic and parsley. Stir-fry for a few minutes and then add the chopped tomatoes.
- Cook over a low heat until the tomato sauce is ready.
- Pour the wine into another pan. Add the raisins, pine nuts and prunes. Cover and cook slowly for about 15 minutes.
- Turn everything into an ovenproof dish: the cod, the tomato sauce and the cooked fruit mixture. Mix carefully with a wooden spoon. Place in a preheated oven for about 15 minutes.
- Serve in the same dish.

Cod with tomato & dried fruits

COD CROQUETTES IN SAUCE

Serves: 6
Difficulty: medium
Required time: 55 minutes

Ingredients:

500 g cured cod (soaked)
1 onion
1 bay leaf
50 g flour
0.5 litre milk
100 g ham
salt
pepper
grated nutmeg
flour for coating fish
oil
1 egg
100 g breadcrumbs

Sauce:

1 onion
parsley
30 g sugar
50 g lard
2 tablesp. vinegar
1.5 dl water

Method:

- Put the cod and bay leaf in a pan covered with cold water. Bring to the boil. Remove from heat and leave to stand, covered, for 20 minutes.
- Remove from water and dab dry. Remove all bones and crush in a mortar.
- Heat oil in a pan and sauté the onion (finely-chopped).
- When the onion is soft, add the flour and allow to brown a little, stirring all the time. Add the milk gradually, ensuring that there are no lumps. Cook until the mixture thickens. Season with salt, pepper and nutmeg. Add the diced ham.
- Add this mixture to the cod.
- Put on a plate to cool.
- When cold, make into croquettes: take a little amount, shape it into a croquette, coat in flour, beaten egg and then breadcrumbs.
- Fry in abundant hot oil.
- Set to one side.

Sauce:

- Melt the lard in an earthenware dish. Fry finely-chopped onion until golden.
- Add chopped parsley. Stir and add the sugar. Remove from heat and add the vinegar and then the water.
- Return pan to heat and bring to boil.
- Cook for a few minutes and add the fried croquettes.
- Heat for a few minutes and serve immediately.

STUFFED SQUID

Serves: 6
Difficulty: medium
Required time: 1 hour 15 minutes

Ingredients:

6 squid (150 – 200 g each)
squid tentacles and fins
100 g small prawns
2 hard boiled eggs
1 egg
2 cloves of garlic
parsley
250 g ripe tomatoes
2 dl white wine
2 dl oil
2 onions
1 carrot
30 g flour
bread crumb soaked in milk
400 g peas (cooked)
1 lemon
25 g pine nuts

Method:

- Clean the squid, leaving them whole.
- Heat a little oil in a pan and stir-fry the prawns. Set to one side.
- In the same oil fry 1 finely-chopped onion. Add the squid tentacles and fins, chopped.
- Remove pan from heat and add the fried prawns, the bread crumb, the chopped garlic and parsley, the 2 hard boiled eggs (chopped) and the raw egg. Mix everything well and use this mixture to fill the squid. Close each squid with a cocktail stick.
- Coat each squid in flour and fry lightly in hot oil.
- Set to one side.
- In the same oil, sauté the other finely-chopped onion. Add the finely-sliced carrot. Pour in the wine and leave to evaporate a little.
- Add the grated tomatoes. Cook for about 10 minutes. Add the flour, stirring, and add a little water. Cook for a few minutes.
- Remove from heat and strain the sauce.
- Put the squid in a heatproof earthenware dish. Add the tomato sauce, the cooked peas and the pine nuts. Cook slowly for about 30 minutes.
- Serve hot, garnished with a lemon sliced in two in the centre and sprinkled with chopped parsley.

STUFFED SQUID, TOSSA-STYLE

Serves: 4
Difficulty: high
Required time: 2 hours

Ingredients:

1 kg small squid
100 g pork loin
4 Golden Delicious apples
3 onions
8 cloves of garlic
6 tablesp. olive oil
50 g lard
50 g butter
1 slice fried bread
4 egg yolks
2 glasses of Port wine
half a glass of red wine
parsley
100 g almonds
2 pieces of chocolate
1 plain biscuit
salt
white pepper

Method:

- Clean the squid, removing tentacles and fins, but leaving them whole.
- Chop tentacles and fins and the pork loin.
- Peel and grate the apples. Separate the egg yolks.
- Heat oil in a pan and sauté the pork and squid. Cover and leave for a few minutes. Remove from heat and stir in the egg yolks and grated apple with a wooden spoon. Season with salt and pepper. Add a glass of Port.
- Crush half the almonds, the fried bread, two cloves of garlic, one piece of chocolate and a pinch of salt.
- Use this mixture to stuff the squid. Place stuffed squid in a heatproof earthenware dish with oil, lard and the onions sliced in rings. Brown and add the red wine and the other glass of Port. When the wine has evaporated, cover with water.
- Prepare another mixture in the same quantities as the filling and add it to the dish. Cook for at least 1 and a half hours.
- Meanwhile, make balls with the same mixture, adding the apple and chopped tentacles and fins. Fry in a separate pan and add them to the earthenware dish 30 minutes before removing dish from heat.
- Before serving, add a little butter and white pepper.

Stuffed squid, Tossa-style

FISH STEW, BARCELONA-STYLE

Serves: 4
Difficulty: high
Required time: 1 hour 15 minutes

Ingredients:

400 g angler
400 g gilthead (or similar)
250 g squid
4 shrimps
4 king prawns
16 mussels
150 g flour
1 onion
3 ripe tomatoes
1 glass of white wine
1.5 dl oil
2 cloves of garlic
parsley
saffron
salt & pepper

Method:

- Cut the angler and gilthead into slices and the squid into rings. Season, coat in flour and fry in hot oil. Once fried, put the pieces into a large heatproof earthenware dish.
- Peel and chop the onions and the tomatoes. Stir-fry the onions and then add the tomatoes. After 2 minutes, add the wine. Allow wine to evaporate and add a little fish stock or water.
- Pour the sauce over the fish in the earthenware dish. Cover and cook over a low heat.
- Crush a few strands of saffron, the parsley and the garlic in a mortar. Mix well, adding a little of the sauce. Add to the dish.
- Cook for 5 minutes in the oven.

FISH STEW, COSTA BRAVA-STYLE

Serves: 4
Difficulty: low
Required time: 50 minutes

Ingredients:

700 g scorpion fish
700 g angler
700 g red sea bream
700 g conger
1.300 kg potatoes
1 dl oil
2 tomatoes
1 onion
3 cloves of garlic
salt

Method:

- Clean the fish, removing heads, tails and bones. Put these into a pan full of salted water to make stock. Cook over a medium heat.
- Peel and cut the potatoes into medium-sized pieces. Peel and chop the onion, garlic and tomatoes and sauté them in hot oil in a heatproof earthenware dish.
- Add the potatoes and the fish. Cover with the fish stock (strained). Turn the heat up and simmer for 20 minutes.

SQUID & SNAIL STEW

Serves: 4
Difficulty: medium
Required time: 45 minutes

Ingredients:

1.200 kg squid
70 snails
2.5 dl oil
2 onions
35 g flour
half a glass of white wine
5 cloves of garlic
15 g pine nuts
2 carquinyolis [see page 158] or other sweet biscuits
dry anisette
salt & pepper

Method:

- Clean the snails in salted water several times. Put them in a pan, cover with water and when the snails start to come out of their shells, remove the latter and turn the heat up. Bring to the boil. Drain the snails and set to one side.
- Wash and clean the squid. Cut into medium-sized pieces.
- Peel and finely cut the garlic into slices and the onions into rings. Heat half the oil in a pan and sauté the onion until golden. Add the squid and then the garlic.
- When golden, add the wine and allow to evaporate. Add the flour and 2 small glasses of water. Mix well and cook over a low heat.
- Season the snails and fry for about 6 minutes in hot oil. Add to the other pan.
- Chop the pine nuts and *carquinyolis* and soak them in the anisette. Add to pan. Check seasoning and cook until the squid is tender.

STEWED CONGER

Serves: 4
Difficulty: low
Required time: 40 minutes (plus soaking time)

Ingredients:

- *600 g cured conger*
- *150 g flour*
- *2.5 dl oil*
- *3 sweet peppers*
- *2 onions*
- *8 tomatoes*
- *2 cloves of garlic*
- *salt*

Method:

- Cut the conger into pieces and soak in water for about 2 hours. Drain well and coat the pieces in flour. Fry in hot oil until golden. Set aside in an earthenware dish.
- Slice the onions and cut peppers into fine strips. Peel and chop the tomatoes. Sauté these ingredients, in the same order, in the same pan. Add half a small glass of water.
- Add this sauce to the fish in the earthenware dish. Cook over a very low heat for about 20 minutes.
- Meanwhile, crush the garlic in a mortar and add oil to make an *allioli* sauce. Add to the earthenware dish. Stir well.

"ESQUEIXADA" (CURED CODFISH SALAD WITH VINAIGRETTE)

Serves: 4
Difficulty: low
Required time: 30 minutes (plus time for soaking cod)

Ingredients:

- *300 g cured cod (thick part)*
- *4 shallots*
- *2 large ripe tomatoes*
- *1.5 dl oil*
- *0.5 dl vinegar*
- *150 g of black and green olives*
- *2 green peppers*
- *2 hard boiled eggs*
- *salt & pepper*

Method:

- Previously desalt the cod (cut into strips) by soaking it 3-4 hours in water, changing the water a couple of times. Dab dry well with a cloth.
- Scald and peel the tomatoes, and deseed them.
- Place the well-drained cod pieces in a serving dish.
- Add the onions (sliced), the tomatoes (cut in wedges), the peppers (cut in rings) and, finally, the olives.
- Prepare a vinaigrette sauce by mixing the oil with the vinegar, salt & pepper very well. Pour vinaigrette over the fish salad.
- Garnish with the sliced hard boiled eggs.
- Serve chilled.

"Esqueixada"

TUNA FISH & SNAIL BEAN STEW

Serves: 4
Difficulty: medium
Required time: 1 hour (plus time for soaking fish and beans)

Ingredients:

- *350 g cured tuna fish*
- *250 g haricot beans*
- *250 g potatoes*
- *50 snails*
- *1 onion*
- *4 tomatoes*
- *1 dl of oil*
- *15 g roasted hazelnuts*
- *3 cloves of garlic*
- *saffron*
- *parsley*
- *salt*

Method:

- Soak the tuna fish and beans in water the evening before.
- Drain the beans and fish and separate them. Cook the beans in salted water.
- Clean the snails in salted water several times. Cook in salted water over a low heat and when the snails start to leave their shells, remove the latter and turn up the heat. Bring to the boil, drain and set to one side.
- Dice the tuna fish.
- Cut the onion into thin rings and chop the tomatoes. Fry them in a little oil. Peel and cut the potatoes into medium-sized pieces.
- Add the (well-drained) snails to the pan with a little of the water used for cooking the beans. Cook for about 20 minutes.
- Add the tuna fish and beans to the pan. Simmer.
- Meanwhile, crush a few strands of saffron, a little parsley, the garlic and the almonds. Add a little of the water from the beans and mix well. Add this mixture to the pan when everything is nearly cooked. Season before serving.

STEWED OCTOPUS WITH CHOCOLATE

Serves: 4
Difficulty: medium
Required time: 45 minutes

Ingredients:

- *800 g octopus*
- *800 g potatoes*
- *1 onion*
- *4 tomatoes*
- *3 cloves of garlic*
- *2.5 dl oil*
- *1 sprig of thyme*
- *1 bay leaf*
- *25 g chocolate*
- *25 g roasted almonds*
- *1 glass of white wine*
- *half a glass of anisette*
- *saffron*
- *salt & pepper*

Method:

- Rinse the octopus in cold water. Boil a little and rinse again under a cold tap. Set to one side.
- Fry the garlic in a heatproof earthenware dish and set aside.

- Peel and finely chop the onion. Peel and cut the potatoes, leaving the small ones whole.
- In the same dish used for frying the garlic, sauté the onion and then add the octopus. Stir-fry for a few minutes and then add the bay leaf, the thyme, the potatoes and the chopped tomatoes. After 3 minutes, pour in the wine and anisette. Season, cover the dish and cook over a slow heat.
- Meanwhile, crush the pieces of chocolate and the fried garlic with the almonds and saffron. Add a little water and mix well. Add to the dish with the octopus. Keep covered and cook until the octopus is tender.

STEWED PRAWNS WITH CHOCOLATE

Serves: 6
Difficulty: medium
Required time: 40 minutes

Ingredients:

600 g king prawns
3 dl oil

Sauce:

2 onions
1 kg tomatoes
1 ham bone
1 bay leaf
thyme
white pepper

Sauce-paste:

3 cloves of garlic
50 g roasted almonds
100 g chocolate
parsley
salt

Method:

- Heat 2 dl of oil in a pan.
- Peel and cut the onions and fry for a few minutes.
- Add the bay leaf, the thyme, the bone and cook until the onion is lightly browned.
- Add the chopped tomatoes (unpeeled) and stir a few times. Cover and cook for 10 minutes.
- Add 1 glass of hot water.
- Cook over a low heat until the sauce thickens.
- When ready, strain the sauce.
- Rinse the prawns, remove their heads, season and fry in the remaining dl of oil.
- Place them in a heatproof earthenware dish.
- Cover them with the sauce.
- Crush the garlic (peeled), almonds, a little parsley and the chocolate in a mortar. Add a little of the oil used for frying the prawns.
- Add this mixture to the dish where the prawns and sauce are. Stir and cook for a few minutes.
- If the sauce is too thick, add a little water.
- Check seasoning.
- Serve hot.

STEWED SQUID WITH CHOCOLATE

Serves: 6
Difficulty: medium
Required time: 1 hour

Ingredients:

600 g squid
1 kg potatoes
1 glass of tomato puree
2.5 dl oil
2 onions
3 cloves of garlic
0.5 litre red wine
1 glass of dry anisette
1 bouquet garni
40 g roasted almonds
1 tablesp. cocoa powder
2 tablesp. fish stock
saffron
salt

Method:

- Clean and cut the squid into rings.
- Peel and fry the garlic in hot oil until golden. Set to one side.
- Peel and chop the onions. Peel the potatoes and cut into pieces.
- Put the chopped onions, the potatoes and the squid rings into the pan in which you fried the garlic. Add the bouquet garni. Season, cover and cook for about 30 minutes.
- Add the tomato puree, the wine and the anisette. A few minutes later, pour in half a litre of water. Cover and cook for a further 15 minutes.
- Meanwhile, crush the almonds, 1 or 2 strands of saffron and the fried cloves of garlic. Blend well. Add the cocoa powder and 2 tablespoons of fish stock. Add this mixture to the pan. Cook for a few minutes.
- Check seasoning and serve.

CONGER STEW

Serves: 4
Difficulty: low
Required time: 40 minutes

Ingredients:

800 g conger
500 g peas
1.5 dl oil
35 g flour
1 small onion
2 cloves of garlic
parsley
salt

Method:

- Cut the conger into large slices.
- Boil the peas in slightly salted water.
- Peel and finely chop the onion. Fry in oil in a heatproof earthenware dish until golden. Add the flour and stir well with a wooden spoon. Add a glass of water (or some the water used to boil the peas). Simmer.
- Drain the peas and add them to the dish with the conger. Add salt and cook over a low heat, stirring occasionally with the wooden spoon.
- Crush the garlic and parsley with a pestle and mortar and add to the dish.
- Cook in the oven until ready.

Stewed squid with chocolate

COD & SPINACH

Serves: 4
Difficulty: medium
Required time: 50 minutes (plus at least 2 hours for soaking)

Ingredients:

- *600 g cured cod*
- *1 kg spinach*
- *150 g flour*
- *100 g raisins*
- *50 g pine nuts*
- *1 small onion*
- *3 cloves of garlic*
- *2.5 dl of oil*
- *salt*

Method:

- Soak the cod (cut in slices) in a bowl of water and the pine nuts and raisins in another for at least 2 hours.
- Wash the spinach, sprinkle with salt and leave to stand for about 30 minutes to "sweat".
- When the cod is desalted, dab dry well and coat in flour. Fry the pieces in a pan in plenty of hot oil. Set to one side.
- Peel and chop the onion. Fry it in a heatproof earthenware dish with a little of the oil used for frying the cod. Add the drained spinach and stir well. When the spinach has shrunk, add the drained pine nuts and raisins.
- Place the cod pieces on top of the spinach. Add half a glass of water, cover and cook until ready.

SQUID & POTATO STEW

Serves: 4
Difficulty: medium
Required time: 45 minutes

Ingredients:

- *600 g squid*
- *800 g potatoes*
- *300 g peas*
- *1 large onion*
- *4 tomatoes*
- *half a glass of Rancio wine*
- *half a glass of anisette*
- *2 cloves of garlic*
- *1.5 dl of oil*
- *15 g pine nuts*
- *saffron*
- *a stick of cinnamon*
- *salt & pepper*

Method:

- Boil the peas. Set to one side
- Wash and dice the squid and sauté in hot oil until golden.
- Whilst the squid is frying, cut the onion into rings and stir-fry it with the squid.
- Peel and dice the tomatoes and add to the squid and onion. Cook for a few minutes.
- Peel and cut the potatoes into medium-sized pieces and add to pan when the squid is half cooked. Add a little water to cover, the cinnamon stick and leave to cook.
- Lightly toast 1 or 2 strands of saffron. Crush them together with the pine nuts and garlic. Add the wine and anisette and mix well. Pour over the squid and add the peas. Season before serving.

Squid & potato stew

LOBSTER, CATALAN-STYLE

Serves: 2
Difficulty: medium
Required time: 35 minutes

Ingredients:

1 large lobster
150 g onions
1 clove of garlic
4 ripe tomatoes
1 dl of oil
ground cinnamon
bay leaf
1 small glass of Rancio wine
salt & pepper

Sauce-paste:

30 g chocolate
50 g roasted almonds
1 sweet biscuit
1 clove of garlic
parsley

Method:

- Peel and finely chop the onion. Heat oil in a heatproof earthenware dish and stir-fry the onion. Add the garlic (chopped) and then the tomatoes (grated). Cook over a low heat.
- Meanwhile, prepare the lobster, slicing it in two lengthwise, removing its stomach. Remove the liver and set aside.
- Cut the lobster into pieces, being careful that the flesh does not come out of the shell, and place the pieces in a pan.
- Sprinkle with cinnamon, salt and pepper and a piece of bay leaf.
- Sprinkle with the wine.

Sauce-paste:

- Crush the almonds, grated chocolate, clove of garlic, parsley and the biscuit with a pestle and mortar. When they are well mixed, blend with a little stock or water. Add to the lobster.
- Cook for about 20 minutes.
- Serve.

LOBSTER WITH SNAILS

Serves: 4
Difficulty: medium
Required time: 1 hour

Ingredients:

1.600 kg lobster
1 kg snails
1 large onion
3 tomatoes
1.5 dl of oil
half a glass of Rancio wine
20 g almonds
1 teasp. crushed hazelnuts
3 cloves of garlic
1 slice of bread
1 bouquet garni (thyme, cinnamon stick, bay leaf and parsley)
saffron
salt

Method:

- Clean the snails in salted water several times. Put them in a pan, cover with water and when the snails start to come out of their shells, remove the latter and turn the heat up. Bring to the boil. Drain the snails and set aside.

- Peel and finely chop the onion. Wash the lobster, slice in two lengthwise, and salt. Peel and chop the tomatoes.
- Heat the oil in a pan and fry the bread. Remove. In the same oil, fry the onion and then the lobster for 5 minutes.
- Add the bouquet garni and the tomatoes. Add a ladle of water, then the snails and cook over a low heat.
- With a pestle and mortar, crush the garlic, the fried bread, almonds, hazelnuts and saffron. Mix well and blend with the wine. Pour this mixture over the lobster in the pan.
- Remove pan from heat when the lobster and snails are cooked.

SEA BASS A LA COSTA BRAVA

Serves: 4
Difficulty: high
Required time: 1 hour 30 minutes

Ingredients:

1 sea bass (whole) weighing approximately 1.300 kg
130 g peas
1 carrot
1 large onion
4 ripe tomatoes
1 sweet pepper
2 cloves of garlic
1.5 dl of oil
2 tablesp. flour
half a glass of white wine
30 g almonds
saffron
1 bay leaf
salt

Method:

- Boil the peas. Roast the pepper and peel it.
- Clean the fish and salt it. Make a few gashes diagonally in the skin so that it will cook better. Place in an oven dish with half the oil and set aside until the sauce is ready.
- Peel and slice the carrot and the onion. Peel and chop the tomatoes.
- Heat the rest of the oil in another pan and add, in the following order: the carrot, the bay leaf and the onion. Fry them. When the onion is nearly brown, add the chopped tomatoes, the wine and cook until the wine is absorbed. Add the flour and blend the sauce with a mixer. Add half a litre of water or fish stock and simmer for 20-30 minutes.
- Crush the saffron, the garlic and add to the sauce in the pan. Cook for a few minutes and then strain the sauce.
- Put the fish in the oven for 10 minutes. Take the dish out of the oven and cover the fish with the sauce, the peas and the peppers. Salt and put the dish back in the oven for a few minutes, making sure that the fish doesn't go dry.

FISH & MEAT STEW, AMPURDÁN-STYLE

Serves: 4
Difficulty: medium
Required time: 50 minutes

Ingredients:

4 prawns
4 king prawns
4 squid
24 mussels
4 sausages
2 pig's trotters
400 g rabbit
4 chicken quarters
40 snails
250 g mushrooms
200 g tomatoes
half an onion
5 cloves of garlic
1 bay leaf
1 sprig of thyme
2 glasses of oil
20 g hazelnuts
20 g almonds
15 g chocolate
half a glass of white wine
half a glass of brandy
salt & pepper

Method:

- Peel and chop the onion, two and a half cloves of garlic and the tomatoes.
- Heat half the oil in a pan and fry the onion, garlic and tomatoes.
- Wash the prawns and squid. Add them to the pan with hot oil along with the chopped rabbit, the chicken quarters, the sausages and the mushrooms.
- Wash the mussels and snails.
- Cook the pig's trotters (split in two lengthwise) in salted water with the thyme and the bay leaf, along with the mussels and the snails. Add them to the pan with the meat.
- Add the brandy (it being recommended to flame it to burn off the alcohol) and turn the heat up.
- Crush the rest of the garlic in a mortar together with the hazelnuts, the almonds, the pine nuts and the chocolate. Mix into a paste. Add the wine and pour the mixture over the meat and fish.
- A little water or fish stock can be added if the sauce becomes too dry. Season with salt and pepper before serving.

Fish & meat stew, Ampurdán-style

MUSSELS, CATALAN-STYLE

Serves: 4
Difficulty: low
Required time: 25 minutes

Ingredients:

1 kg mussels (if possible, rock mussels)
2 dl of olive oil
1 large onion
2 ripe tomatoes
1 clove of garlic
2 dl of dry white wine
parsley
salt & pepper

Method:

- Scrape and wash the mussels well.
- Steam open the mussels. After a few minutes, sprinkle them with a little of the wine.
- Strain the mussel stock and remove the mussels.
- Fry the finely-chopped onion in a pan. Add the peeled, chopped and deseeded tomatoes, the chopped clove of garlic and parsley. Pour the strained mussel stock into the pan. Cook over a low heat.
- When the sauce is nearly ready, add the rest of the wine. Let it cook until absorbed a little.
- Add the mussels and cook for about 5 minutes.
- Serve garnished with finely-chopped parsley.

HAKE WITH PINE NUTS

Serves: 4
Difficulty: low
Required time: 30 minutes

Ingredients:

4 thick slices of hake

Sauce:

2 cloves of garlic
2 ripe tomatoes
100 g pine nuts
1 dl of dry white wine
1 glass of water
half a lemon
half a bay leaf
olive oil
salt
parsley
white pepper

Method:

- Roast the tomatoes and cloves of garlic over the flame. Peel and crush them in the mortar. Add the pine nuts. Crush well (can also be done with a mixer). Add the white wine and a little water.
- Put a little oil into a heatproof earthenware dish. Add the above-mentioned ingredients. Season and add the bay leaf.
- Cook for about 10 minutes over a low heat until the sauce has been absorbed a little.
- Add the slices of hake sprinkled with the lemon juice. Cover and cook for 10 minutes over a low heat.
- Serve garnished with finely-chopped parsley.

Hake with pine nuts

OVEN BAKED GROUPER, AMPURDÁN-STYLE

Serves: 4
Difficulty: low
Required time: 50 minutes

Ingredients:

1.200 g grouper
1 large onion
1.5 dl of oil
1 tablesp. vinegar
3 cloves of garlic
parsley
salt & pepper

Method:

- Clean and chop the fish into round slices. Peel and cut the onion into rings.
- Place the fish on a greased oven tray, together with the onion, the chopped garlic and parsley and sprinkle with oil.
- Season with salt and pepper, cover with aluminium foil and bake in oven. When half-cooked, turn the fish and add a little water mixed with the vinegar.
- When ready, remove from oven and put the fish on a serving dish.
- Just before serving, pour the sauce over.

SMOKED COD

Serves: 6
Difficulty: medium
Required time: 1 hour (plus 4 days for soaking)

Ingredients:

1.200 g cured smoked cod
2 kg potatoes
4 tomatoes
2 onions
4 cloves of garlic
40 g hazelnuts
2 carquinyolis [see page 158] or other sweet biscuits
1 dl of oil
saffron
salt

Method:

- Dry the cod well and cut into 12 pieces.
- Peel and chop the onion. Grate the tomatoes. Heat oil in a frying pan and fry both.
- Peel and cut the potatoes. Add them to the frying pan. After 5 minutes, add the cod and cover with water. Cook gently over a low heat.
- Meanwhile, toast the strands of saffron. Crush them in a mortar together with the garlic, hazelnuts, almonds and biscuits. Mix with a little of the juice from the sauce, stir well and add to the pan a few minutes before removing the pan from the heat.

Oven-baked grouper, Ampurdán-style

MIXED FISH IN ROMESCO SAUCE

Serves: 4
Difficulty: high
Required time: 1 hour 20 minutes

Ingredients:

4 slices of angler
4 slices of dentex (or similar)
4 large shrimps
4 king prawns
600 g lobster
20 mussels
2 onions
4 tomatoes
3 cloves of garlic
150 g flour
1 glass of white wine
3 dl of oil
salt

Garnish:

2 dried peppers
50 g roasted almonds
2 cloves of garlic
1 slice of bread
parsley
salt
chilli
pepper

Method:

- Soak the deseeded dried peppers in warm water for about 2 hours.
- Heat the oil in a pan and fry the bread until golden. Set to one side.
- Season and coat the fish in flour. Fry the fish in the same oil used for frying the bread. When the fish is golden, remove from pan and place in a large heatproof earthenware dish. Add the shellfish.
- In the same oil, sauté the finely-chopped onion. When it starts to turn brown, add the 3 cloves of garlic (chopped) and the grated tomatoes.
- When the sauce is nearly ready, add the wine and let it evaporate. Add a little water or fish stock and cook gently for 5 minutes.
- Season.
- Pour the sauce over the fish.

Garnish:

- Crush the almonds, the (previously-roasted and peeled) 2 cloves of garlic, the fried bread, the chilli, parsley, salt and pulp of the peppers. Mix well and blend with a little of the tomato sauce. Add to the fish in the dish, cover and cook for about 15 minutes.
- Remove from heat and leave to stand for a few minutes.

Mixed fish in romesco sauce

OCTOPUS WITH TOMATO & ONION

Serves: 4
Difficulty: low
Required time: 45 minutes

Ingredients:

900 g octopus
2 onions
400 g ripe tomatoes
6 cloves of garlic
1 glass of dry white wine
1.5 dl of oil
parsley
salt & pepper

Method:

- Clean the octopus. Peel and finely chop the onions. Scald the tomatoes in boiling water to remove skin, then chop them finely. Peel and slice the garlic.
- Prepare a heatproof earthenware dish with oil. Put in the octopus and all the other ingredients (raw). Pour over the wine. Cover and cook very gently over a low heat.
- After a while, check that the juice from the octopus is being absorbed. Season.
- Leave to cook for a while longer.
- Check seasoning.
- Serve in the same dish garnished with chopped parsley.

ANGLER, CATALAN-STYLE

Serves: 4
Difficulty: low
Required time: 45 minutes

Ingredients:

1 kg angler (skinless fillets)
3 cloves of garlic
1 large onion
50 g grated chocolate
1 tablesp. vinegar
1 bay leaf
200 g flour
quarter litre of oil
1 ladle of fish stock/water
parsley
salt & pepper

Method:

- Salt the fillets, coat them in flour and fry in hot oil.
- When they are golden, place them in a large heatproof earthenware dish.
- Peel and finely chop the onion and put it on top of the fish. Add the whole cloves of garlic (peeled), the vinegar, the bay leaf, the grated chocolate and the oil from frying the fish. Add the ladle of stock/water.
- Cover and cook gently over a low heat for about 30 minutes.
- Serve in the same dish garnished with chopped parsley.

Angler, Catalan-style

ANGLER MATELOTE

Serves: 4
Difficulty: low
Required time: 45 minutes

Ingredients:

800 g angler (cut in 8 pieces)
2.5 dl of oil
salt & pepper

Sauce:

2 slices of bread
2 ripe tomatoes
1 clove of garlic
1 glass of dry white wine
2 dried peppers
100 g roasted almonds
saffron
chopped parsley

Method:

- Heat the oil in a heatproof earthenware dish and fry the bread. Remove from pan and put it in a mortar. Fry the garlic, tomatoes, almonds and saffron, taking them out when golden and adding them to the mortar.
- Crush all the ingredients in the mortar and mix well into a paste. Blend with the wine and pour the mixture back into the pan.
- Add the angler and enough water to barely cover the fish.
- Cook over a low heat for about 20 minutes.
- Serve in the same dish, garnished with chopped parsley.

Suggestion:

Five minutes before the fish is fully cooked some clams may be added.

ANGLER "A L'ALL CREMAT"

Serves: 4
Difficulty: medium
Required time: 1 hour

Ingredients:

1 kg angler (in slices)
6 cloves of garlic
1 large ripe tomato
1.5 dl of oil
1 kg potatoes
4 thin slices of bread
1 bay leaf
a little chilli
parsley
salt & pepper
7 dl fish stock

Fish stock:

1 litre of water
400 g fish heads and bones
half an onion
mushroom stalks
1 small glass of white wine
parsley
salt

Method:

- Make the stock by boiling all its ingredients for about 20 minutes in a covered pan.
- Strain and set to one side.
- Heat the oil in a frying pan. Peel and slice the garlic and fry until dark brown, almost burnt (but not black, as this would make the sauce bitter).
- Remove the garlic and fry the bread in the same oil. Add the bay leaf, the parsley and the chilli.
- Put this fried mixture into a mortar, leaving some oil in the pan. Mix the ingredients well.
- Stir-fry the tomatoes in the remaining oil.
- Turn the mortar mixture back into the pan with the tomatoes and stir carefully until the sauce is a dark colour (known as "chocolate" by local fishermen).
- When the sauce is ready, add the stock (hot).
- Cook, covered, for about 5 minutes.
- Add the diced potatoes and when half-cooked the fish. Season.
- Turn heat up and finish cooking the fish.
- Serve hot.

Suggestion:

Soft fish can also be used (hake, mackerel or sardines). In this case, add the fish when the potatoes are fully cooked and don't stir. Cook for about 5 minutes.

ANGLER "A L'ALL CREMAT", GIRONA-STYLE

Serves: 4
Difficulty: medium
Required time: 55 minutes

Ingredients:

1 kg angler
4 large prawns
4 tomatoes
5 cloves of garlic
0.5 litre of fish stock
2 dl of oil
4 slices of bread
1 bay leaf
parsley
half a small chilli
salt & pepper

Method:

- Remove the head from the angler and cut the fish into 4 pieces. Season with salt and pepper and coat in flour.
- Make the fish stock by boiling a little more than half a litre of water with the fish head. Keep it hot.
- Peel and slice the garlic. Cut the tomatoes in half and deseed them.
- Heat half the oil in a frying pan and fry the garlic until very brown (but not burnt) and remove from pan. Add the bread, parsley, chilli and bay leaf to the same oil. Sauté them a little.
- Discard the bay leaf and turn the rest of the ingredients (leaving the oil in the frying pan) into a mortar together with the fried garlic. Blend well into a smooth paste.
- Fry the tomatoes in the remaining oil. Add the paste and pour in the stock. Stir well and simmer for about 20 minutes.
- Fry the fish pieces (coated in flour) in another pan with the other half of the oil (hot). Drain the fish well and place the pieces in a casserole dish along with the prawns and the sauce.
- Bake in a hot oven for a few minutes, making sure that the fish does not get overcooked.

Angler "a l'all cremat", Girona-style

RAY FISH WITH PEAS

Serves: 4
Difficulty: medium
Required time: 55 minutes

Ingredients:

1.300 kg ray fish
250 g peas
150 g flour
1 small onion
2 cloves of garlic
parsley
salt & pepper
1.5 ladles of fish stock

Method:

- Rinse the fish with cold water and scald it in boiling water. Keep this stock. With a sharp knife remove the skin from the fish and cut it into pieces. Salt the fish, coat it in flour and fry it in a little oil until golden. Set to one side.
- In another pan, boil the peas.
- Peel and finely chop the onion. Sauté it until golden in a heatproof earthenware dish with the rest of the oil. Add a little less than a tablespoonful of flour, stir it in well and pour in nearly all the stock.
- Place the fish pieces in the middle of the dish and the drained peas on top of the fish. Cover and cook for a few minutes.
- Meanwhile, crush the garlic and parsley with a pestle and mortar and blend them well together with a little of the fish stock. Pour over the fish. Season before putting in the oven for a few minutes.

RED MULLET, CATALAN-STYLE

Serves: 4
Difficulty: low
Required time: 30 minutes

Ingredients:

4 large red mullets
3 cloves of garlic
2 ripe tomatoes
25 g breadcrumbs
2 dl of olive oil
1 dl of dry white wine
parsley
salt & pepper

Method:

- Clean the fish and, with a sharp knife, make a few diagonal cuts on each.
- Scald, peel and chop the tomatoes. Peel and chop the garlic.
- Place the fish on a greased oven tray. Season with salt and pepper and sprinkle with the chopped garlic and parsley, the chopped tomatoes and breadcrumbs.
- Drizzle with the oil and wine and bake in a preheated oven for 20-25 minutes until cooked (when the fish eyes turn white).
- Serve immediately.

Red mullet, Catalan-style

MARINATED SARDINES

Serves: 4
Difficulty: low
Required time: 30 minutes

Ingredients:

20 large sardines
quarter litre of oil
150 g flour
6 cloves of garlic
bay leaf
1 sprig of thyme
quarter litre of vinegar
1 tablesp. paprika
salt

Method:

- Clean the sardines well. Rinse, dab dry, salt and coat in flour.
- Heat the oil in a frying pan. Fry the sardines until golden. Remove the sardines to an earthenware dish, leaving the oil in the frying pan.
- In the same oil, sauté the chopped garlic, the thyme and the bay leaf.
- Let the oil cool a little and add the paprika and the vinegar, being careful that the paprika does not burn.
- Cook for a few minutes and then pour over the sardines. Leave to cool.
- Best eaten 3-4 days later.

CUTTLEFISH WITH MEATBALLS

Serves: 4
Difficulty: medium
Required time: 1 hour 15 minutes

Ingredients:

300 g minced veal
100 g minced pork
1 egg
1 clove of garlic
1 slice of bread
a little milk
1 onion
200 g ripe tomatoes
100 g flour
1 bouquet garni
quarter litre of stock
quarter litre of red wine
600 g cuttlefish
25 g pine nuts
half a teasp. ground cinnamon
1 tablesp. flour
a few slices of toast
parsley
oil

Method:

- Mix the mince. Add the chopped garlic and parsley, the bread soaked in milk and the egg (slightly beaten). Mix well together with a fork. Season and add a little cinnamon.
- Shape this mixture into balls. Coat each ball in flour and fry in plenty hot oil.
- Set to one side.
- Clean and chop the cuttlefish. Cook in a small pan, covered, with the wine for about 15 minutes.
- In the oil used for frying the meatballs, sauté the finely-chopped onion.

- When it starts to go brown, add the sauce left from cooking the cuttlefish. Add 1 tablespoonful of flour. When it browns, add the tomatoes (chopped but *not* peeled), the bouquet garni and the stock. Cover and cook for about 15 minutes.
- Strain the sauce well.
- Put the meatballs and the cuttlefish in an earthenware oven dish and pour the sauce over. Cover and cook in the oven (at 180°C) for about 20 minutes. When half-cooked, add the pine nuts (previously soaked).
- Serve in the same dish, garnished with toast.

CUTTLEFISH WITH CABBAGE

Serves: 6
Difficulty: medium
Required time: 1 hour

Ingredients:

1.5 kg cuttlefish
500 g lean mince
2 cabbages
2 kg tomatoes
2 onions
100 g flour
50 g lard
1 head of garlic
2 dl of oil
1 glass of white wine
1 bay leaf
grated nutmeg
salt & pepper

Method:

- Peel and cut the onions into rings. Peel and chop the tomatoes. Scald the cuttlefish in boiling water and cut into medium-sized pieces. Wash the cabbage leaves and boil for 2-3 minutes.
- Dry the cabbage leaves on a cloth and season with salt, pepper and grated nutmeg.
- Melt the lard in a frying pan and sauté the onion. Add the tomatoes, the head of garlic, the bay leaf and the wine. When the wine is absorbed, remove pan from heat.
- Salt the mince and fill the cabbage leaves with it, rolling them up with the mince inside, making sure they are tightly closed.
- Coat each roll in flour and fry in hot oil in another pan. Remove from the pan and set aside.
- In the same oil, fry the cuttlefish and then add it to the pan with the tomato sauce. Put the cabbage rolls on top. Add 2-3 glasses of water. Cover and cook for at least half an hour. Remove the garlic, bay leaf and serve.

CUTTLEFISH & BEAN STEW

Serves: 4
Difficulty: high
Required time: 50 minutes (plus soaking time for beans)

Ingredients:

- *350 g cuttlefish*
- *400 g haricot beans*
- *1 large onion*
- *4 tomatoes*
- *3 cloves of garlic*
- *1 green pepper*
- *1.5 dl of oil*
- *saffron*
- *salt*

Method:

- Soak the beans in water at least 6 hours before starting.
- Put the beans in a pan, covered with cold water and bring to the boil. Cook over a high heat.
- Wash and dice the cuttlefish. Set to one side.
- Chop the pepper and peel and chop the onion. Fry them in oil in a heatproof earthenware dish until golden. Add the cuttlefish.
- Peel, deseed and chop the tomatoes. Add them to the pan and fry. Add a glass of the water used to boil the beans. Cook for 5 minutes.
- Meanwhile, crush the garlic and a few strands of saffron with a pestle and mortar.
- When the beans are nearly ready, add the cuttlefish, tomato sauce and the crushed garlic and saffron to their pan.

"SIMI-TOMBA", AMPURDÁN-STYLE (COD & MUSHROOM STEW)

Serves: 4
Difficulty: medium
Required time: 50 minutes

Ingredients:

- *1 kg cod*
- *300 g mushrooms*
- *6 potatoes*
- *1 onion*
- *6 cloves of garlic*
- *6 tablesp. oil*
- *fish stock*
- *vinegar*
- *pinch of sugar*

Method:

- Cut the cod into pieces and fry in oil together with the mushrooms. Remove from pan and set aside.
- Peel and cut the onion, the potatoes and thickly-slice 4 cloves of garlic. Add to the same oil in the pan and stir-fry for a few minutes. Cover and cook gently over a low heat. Add the stock and turn the heat up. Simmer for about 30 minutes. Add the cod and mushrooms.
- Stir occasionally and add a few drops of vinegar, a little cold oil and the sugar. Stir until it boils and remove the pan from the heat.
- Meanwhile, prepare a thick *allioli* sauce [see page 5] with the rest of the garlic and oil. Add it to the pan with the cod and stir in well.

Cuttlefish & bean stew

"SIMI-TOMBA" (SHARK/DOGFISH STEW)

Serves: 4
Difficulty: high
Required time: 1 hour

Ingredients:

900 g shark/dogfish
1 kg potatoes
1 and a half onions
2.5 dl of oil
4 cloves of garlic
1 fish stock cube
salt

Method:

- Scald the fish for 1 minute in boiling water to prevent it from giving a bitter taste to the stew. Remove skin and cut into pieces.
- Peel and finely-chop onion and 2 cloves of garlic. Peel and cut the potatoes in medium-sized pieces. Put them all into a heatproof earthenware dish with just over 1 dl of oil and fry.
- Dissolve the stock cube in a glass of warm water and add to the dish.
- When the potatoes are half-cooked, add the fish and salt.
- Make an *allioli* sauce with the rest of the oil and garlic. Add 2 spoonfuls of the sauce to the dish 5 minutes before removing from the heat.

ANCHOVY "SUQUET"

Serves: 4
Difficulty: low
Required time: 40 minutes

Ingredients:

1 kg fresh anchovies
600 g potatoes
1 onion
5 ripe tomatoes
1 head of garlic
bread
oil
pepper & salt

Sauce-paste:

1 slice of bread
10 roasted almonds
1 teasp. flour
4 cloves of garlic
parsley
salt

Method:

- Heat the oil in a heatproof earthenware dish and fry the bread. Remove and set aside.
- In the same oil, sauté the finely-chopped onion, the head of garlic and the tomatoes (deseeded and chopped). Add a little water and the potatoes (peeled and sliced in rounds).
- Cook over a low heat.
- When the potatoes are half cooked, add the anchovies (previously cleaned and seasoned).
- Meanwhile, make a paste by crushing the fried bread, almonds, 4 cloves of garlic and parsley with a pestle and mortar. Add 1

teasp. of flour and a little water. Mix well to blend.

- Pour over the fish and potatoes. Check seasoning and serve.

COD & PRAWN "SUQUET"

Serves: 4
Difficulty: medium
Required time: 1 hour 15 minutes (plus time for soaking cod)

Ingredients:

4 pieces of cured cod (desalted) weighing 150 g each
12 prawns
8 tomatoes
1 onion
6 potatoes
olive oil

Sauce-paste:

12 roasted almonds
1 hard boiled egg
1 clove of garlic
parsley
2 small slices of toast
oil

Method:

- Dab the cod dry with a cloth. Coat in flour and fry in oil. Set to one side.
- Peel the potatoes and leave them in water to release the starch.
- In the oil used for frying the fish, fry the finely-chopped onion. Add the coarsely-chopped tomatoes.
- Add the potatoes (thickly-sliced in rounds), stir-fry a little and cover barely with hot water.
- Crush all the ingredients of the sauce-paste with a pestle and mortar and mix well to a paste. Add this to the pan with the potatoes.
- Cook over a low heat for about 10 minutes.
- Add the prawns and cook for a further 5 minutes.
- When ready, remove the pan from heat and add the cod pieces (already fried). Leave to stand for 30 minutes so that the fish will absorb the flavour of the sauce.
- Re-heat for a few minutes, making sure that the fish pieces do not break. Serve.

MIXED FISH "SUQUET"

Serves: 4
Difficulty: medium
Required time: 50 minutes

Ingredients:

4 thick slices of angler
4 slices of gilthead
4 slices of scorpion fish
4 large shrimps
8 mussels
500 g potatoes
1 onion
half a litre of stock/water
2 dl of olive oil
1 dl of white wine
a few drops of liquor
salt

"Allioli" sauce:

125 ml oil
4 cloves of garlic

Sauce-paste:

angler liver
50 g roasted almonds
1 tablesp. flour
1 slice of bread
3 cloves of garlic
chilli
parsley
saffron
1 teasp. sweet paprika

Method:

- Clean and salt all the fish.
- Scrape the mussels.
- Heat the olive oil in a heatproof earthenware dish and fry the garlic and the slice of bread until golden. Remove them from the pan and fry the liver.
- Crush the fried bread, the almonds, the fried garlic, the liver, the chilli, the parsley and saffron (toasted) with a pestle and mortar.
- Add the paprika, 1 spoonful of flour and a little of the oil from frying the bread and garlic.
- Mix well and pour into the earthenware dish. Cook over a slow heat. Add the fish stock/water and the diced potatoes.
- When half-cooked, add all the fish
- Check seasoning.
- Sprinkle with the wine and liquor.
- Add the shrimps and mussels. Cover and cook for about 15 minutes.
- Make the *allioli* sauce with the pestle and mortar, by crushing the garlic and adding the oil gradually. Mix well.
- Add the *allioli* to the earthenware dish and shake to extend it evenly.
- Serve in the same dish.

Mixed fish "suquet"

STUFFED BAKED TROUT

Serves: 4
Difficulty: low
Required time: 50 minutes

Ingredients:

- *4 trout, weighing 200 g each*
- *200 g white fish fillet (hake or similar)*
- *4 slices of cured ham*
- *250 g new carrots*
- *1 egg yolk*
- *2 egg whites*
- *1 tablesp. chopped chives*
- *1 lemon*
- *1 dl of dry sherry*
- *0.5 dl of cream*
- *parsley*
- *salt & pepper*

Sauce:

- *2 dl cream*
- *40 sultanas*
- *1 dl of juice from cooking the trout*

Method:

- Cut open the trout on the back and remove the bones. Rinse well. Season with salt and pepper and sprinkle with lemon juice.
- Chop the fillets of white fish and mix well with the egg yolk and cream. Add the finely-chopped chives and parsley. Season.
- Whisk the egg whites until stiff and carefully stir them into the previous mixture.
- Fill the trout with this mixture, flattening them. If necessary, sew them up.
- Sprinkle with the sherry and 1 dl of water.
- Place the trout on a greased oven tray with the sliced carrot. Bake in a preheated oven at 180ºC for about 25 minutes.
- When the trout are ready, remove the skin before placing on an ovenproof serving dish.

Sauce:

- Take the juice from baking the trout and mix it in a small pan with the sultanas and cream. Cook over a low heat until a smooth cream.
- Drizzle this sauce over the trout and grill in the oven for about 5 minutes.
- Serve hot.

"SARSUELA" (FISH AND SHELLFISH STEW)

Serves: 6
Difficulty: high
Required time: 1 hour 15 minutes

Ingredients:

- *6 slices of angler*
- *6 slices of gilthead, grouper (or any other similar fish)*
- *6 slices of hake or whiting*
- *6 large shrimps*
- *6 king prawns*
- *24 mussels or clams*
- *400 g of squid (cut in rings)*
- *1 large onion*
- *1 bay leaf*
- *3 ripe tomatoes*
- *1.5 dl of dry white wine*
- *2 dl of olive oil*
- *1 lemon*

salt & pepper

Sauce:

2 small slices of bread
2 cloves of garlic
25 g of roasted almonds
a few strands of saffron (slightly toasted)
parsley
salt

Method:

- Clean the fish well and season.
- When the mussels are clean, steam them open in a pan, covered.
- Drizzle with a little wine and remove one half of each shell. Strain the juice and set aside.
- Fry the bread in hot oil. Remove and put it in a mortar.
- Using the same oil, sauté the shrimps and prawns. Remove from pan. Then sauté the squid and remove from pan.
- Coat the fish in flour and fry it lightly in the same oil. Place the fish pieces in a large earthenware dish, spacing them out. Add the squid rings, the shrimps and prawns (on top and in between).
- In the other pan, in the same oil, sauté the finely-chopped onion. Add the grated tomatoes and the bay leaf. When the tomatoes are cooked, add the rest of the wine. Cook until the wine has been nearly all absorbed.
- Add the juice from opening the mussels and a little water or fish stock. Boil for a few minutes and pour it over the ingredients (barely covering them) in the earthenware dish. Cover and cook for 10 minutes.
- Meanwhile, with a pestle and mortar, crush the fried bread, roasted almonds, toasted saffron, the parsley and salt. Mix well into a smooth paste. Dilute with a little of the fish sauce and check seasoning. Add salt and pepper if necessary.
- Remove the bay leaf and pour the almond sauce over the fish.
- Put the earthenware dish into a preheated oven (200°C) and cook, uncovered, for about 10 minutes (until the fish is ready).
- Serve in the same dish.
- Just before serving, drizzle with lemon juice and sprinkle with chopped parsley.

Suggestion:

Any kind of fish can be used to make this dish. It can also be made just with shellfish.

One of the most popular ways of cooking meat in Catalonia is braising, almost directly over the flame. There are also traditional roasts, veal or lamb stews, but also rabbit with "allioli", chicken, duck with beans, roast turkey and delicious stuffings. Butifarra and other types of sausages are widely used to accompany a variety of other dishes.

STEWED LAMB´S LIVER

Serves: 4
Difficulty: medium
Required time: 50 minutes

Ingredients:

200 g lamb's liver
200 g lamb's lungs
200 g lamb's heart
3 tomatoes
2 onions
2 peppers
4 cloves of garlic
2 small glasses of fresh coagulated blood
2.5 dl of oil, salt & pepper
30 g roasted almonds
half a glass of Rancio wine
half a glass of white wine
half a glass of dry anisette
2 carquinyolis *[see page 158]* *or other sweet biscuits*

Method:

- Chop the liver, lungs and heart. Fry it all in a pan with a little oil. Set to one side.
- Peel and chop the onion and 3 cloves of garlic. Chop the pepper. Peel and grate the tomatoes.
- Heat the rest of the oil in another pan and sauté the onion, garlic and pepper. Add the tomatoes and season. Cut the blood into pieces. Set to one side.
- Add the liver etc. to the tomato base as well as the wine, anisette and blood. Add a little water and turn the heat up.
- Peel and chop the remaining clove of garlic. Crush the *carquinyolis* and almonds. Mix them with water and add to the pan. Cook gently over a slow heat.

BEEF, PYRENEES-STYLE

Serves: 4
Difficulty: low
Required time: 50 minutes

Ingredients:

1 round of beef with rump and shank, weighing 1.200 kg
100 g lard
4 tomatoes
1 large onion
1 head of garlic
half a glass of Rancio wine
half a glass of liquor
2 cloves
1 cinnamon stick
salt & pepper

Method:

- Season the meat and tie it with butcher's string. Put it in a pan on the cooker.
- Melt the lard in another pan and pour it over the meat.
- Peel and chop the onion and tomatoes in medium-sized pieces and sauté them in the same pan. A few minutes later add the wine, the liquor, the cloves and a glass of water. Cover with aluminium foil and cook gently over a low heat.
- When the meat is cooked, remove the foil and cut the string. Slice the meat and put the slices back into the pan with the sauce. Heat for a few minutes and serve.

Beef, Pyrenees-style

SWEET BUTIFARRA SAUSAGE, AMPURDÁN-STYLE

Serves: 6
Difficulty: low
Required time: 20 minutes

Ingredients:

6 sweet butifarra sausages
1 glass of muscatel wine
3 tablesp. sugar
rind of 1 lemon
1 stick of cinnamon
a few slices of toast

Method:

- Place the sausages in a shallow earthenware dish and prick them with a fork.
- Cover them barely with water. Add the muscatel, sugar, cinnamon and lemon rind.
- Cook gently over a low heat until the liquid thickens like a syrup.
- Add a few slices of toast to soak up the syrup and serve on top of the butifarra sausages.
- Serve immediately, hot.

Suggestion:

Since this is a sweet dish it may also be eaten as a dessert.

VEAL TRIPE, CATALAN-STYLE

Serves: 4
Difficulty: medium
Required time: 55 minutes

Ingredients:

800 g tripe
900 g potatoes
4 tomatoes
3 onions
4 cloves of garlic
0.5 litre of oil
1 glass of white wine
parsley
salt
ground pepper

Method:

- Cut the tripe into strips, rinse and cook in a pan with water.
- Peel and slice the onion into thin rings. Peel and grate the tomatoes. Cut the potatoes into sticks and set aside.
- Heat 1 dl of oil in a frying pan. Sauté the onions and then add the cooked tripe. Turn the heat down and add the tomatoes.
- When the tomatoes are cooked, add the wine. When the wine has been absorbed, add a little water. Season with salt and pepper.
- Heat the rest of the oil in another frying pan. Fry the potatoes. Drain and add to the pan. Stir. Peel and chop the garlic and parsley.
- When cooked, turn into another shallow dish for serving. Sprinkle with the chopped garlic and parsley. Put into the oven until golden brown.

"CAP I POTA" WITH TRIPE (STEWED VEAL AND TRIPE)

Serves: 4
Difficulty: medium
Required time: 1 hour

Ingredients:

- *350 g calf's head*
- *350 g calf's tripe*
- *3 legs of veal*
- *1 large onion*
- *4 tomatoes*
- *4 cloves of garlic*
- *2.5 dl of oil*
- *half a glass of Rancio wine*
- *15 g pine nuts*
- *2 slices of fried bread*
- *half a carrot*
- *half a leek*
- *1 bay leaf*
- *thyme*
- *salt*
- *grains of pepper*

Method:

- If possible, buy the tripe, head and legs half-cooked. Put them in a pan of cold water together with the bay leaf, thyme, carrot and leek. Season and cook until soft.
- Keep a little of this stock. Remove the bones from the legs and head and dice the meat.
- Chop the onion and peel and chop the tomatoes.
- Heat the oil in an earthenware dish and fry the garlic, slices of bread and pine nuts. Then crush them all with a pestle and mortar. Add the wine. Set to one side.
- In the same pan, sauté the meat and tripe. Drain well, remove from pan and fry the onions and tomatoes in the same oil.
- After about 10 minutes, when the tomato sauce is ready, add the meat and tripe, a glass of stock and the mixture made previously in the mortar.
- Cook for about 20 minutes. Check seasoning before serving.

"CAP I POTA" WITH PEPPERS (STEWED VEAL WITH PEPPERS)

Serves: 4
Difficulty: medium
Required time: 1 hour (plus 1 hour for draining the aubergines)

Ingredients:

400 g leg of veal (already cooked)
400 g calf's head (already cooked)
2 raw butifarra sausages
2 red peppers
3 green peppers
chilli
500 g ripe tomatoes
3 aubergines
2 onions
60 g flour
1 dl of dry sherry
2 dl of water
3 cloves of garlic
parsley
salt
pepper

Method:

- Heat the oil in a large pan and sauté the diced onions and red peppers. Cook a little and add the green peppers (diced) and a little chilli. Cook for 5 minutes.
- Add the diced aubergines (previously peeled, salted and left to drain 1 hour). Stir carefully, add the sherry and cook until the sherry has been absorbed.
- Add the tomatoes, peeled and finely-chopped. Cook for a few minutes and then sprinkle in the flour. Cook a few minutes more until the mixture starts to turn brown.
- Add a glass of warm water and cook very gently for 10 minutes.
- In another large pan/dish, arrange the veal cut into pieces and the raw butifarra sausage (skinless and slightly mashed).
- Pour the sauce from the other pan over the meat, stirring carefully. Add a little freshly-ground pepper and cook for a further 20 minutes, over a very low heat.
- Serve hot in the same pan/dish garnished with a little chopped parsley.

"Cap i pota" with peppers

PORK CHOPS WITH CHESTNUTS

Serves: 4
Difficulty: low
Required time: 50 minutes (plus one day for soaking the chestnuts)

Ingredients:

- *500 g pork chops*
- *500 g chestnuts*
- *4 tomatoes*
- *1 onion*
- *1 dl of oil*
- *rind of 1 lemon*
- *salt*
- *sugar*

Method:

- The day before, put the chestnuts in water.
- Drain and peel the chestnuts.
- Peel and chop the onion and tomatoes.
- Heat the oil in a pan and lightly fry the chops. Add the onion, and, when it is brown, the tomatoes. Cook for a few minutes, then cover with water.
- Cook over a low heat until it reaches boiling point. Add the lemon rind and chestnuts. Turn heat up.
- Caramelise the sugar, and, 10 minutes before serving, add it to the pan.
- Check seasoning and serve.

LAMB CHOPS WITH HAM

Serves: 4
Difficulty: low
Required time: 40 minutes

Ingredients:

- *8 lamb chops*
- *800 g fresh ham (in large slices)*
- *700 g potatoes*
- *150 g breadcrumbs*
- *150 g flour*
- *1 and a half onions*
- *half a litre of oil and salt*
- *2 eggs*
- *70 g pine nuts*
- *half a glass of white wine*

Method:

- Peel and cut the potatoes into rounds and the onions into rings.
- Salt the chops and fry them lightly in oil.
- Separate the eggs, and beat the yolks on a plate. Put the flour on another plate and the breadcrumbs on a third.
- Wrap each chop in a slice of ham. Coat the chops in flour, egg and breadcrumbs. Fry again until golden brown. Remove from pan.
- In the same oil, fry the potatoes. Remove from pan, drain well, season and place in an oven dish.
- Fry the onions and, when almost brown, add salt and the pine nuts. Stir and add to the potatoes in the dish.
- Pour over the wine and add the chops. Cook in a hot oven for 5 minutes.
- Serve hot.

Lamb chops with ham

HARE "CIVET" (STEWED MARINATED HARE)

Serves: 6
Difficulty: high
Required time: 2 hour 30 minutes (plus time for marinating)

Ingredients:

1 hare
100 g lean bacon
quarter litre of stock
3 tablesp. flour
1 onion
1 carrot
3 cloves of garlic
vanilla chocolate
salt
pepper

Marinade:

1 onion
1 carrot
quarter litre of white wine
half a litre of red wine
1 dl of olive oil
1 clove
1 bouquet garni (thyme, bay leaf and parsley)
ground black pepper

Sauce:

200 g shallots
200 g mushrooms

Garnish:

parsley
fried bread or toast

Method:

- Prepare the marinade in a large bowl with the hare (cleaned and chopped, keeping the liver), the chopped shallot and carrot, the herbs, the clove, the pepper, the oil and the wines.
- Leave to marinate in a cool, dry place for about 12 hours.
- After this time, fry the finely-chopped bacon and the sliced onion. After a while, add the finely-chopped carrot. Stir-fry.
- Add the flour, stirring well until lightly browned. Add the hare (well-drained and dried with a cloth).
- Fry a little until brown, making sure that it does not stick to the pan.
- Pour in the wines and simmer gently (uncovered). Add a little stock, the chopped garlic and the bouquet garni. Cover and cook over a low heat for approximately 1 hour.
- Cook the liver for a few minutes.
- Put the hare into another pan. Strain the sauce from cooking the hare and pour over the hare. Crush the liver and chocolate with a pestle and mortar. Dilute with a little of the sauce, mix well and add to the pan.
- In another pan, sauté the shallots, add a little water and cook (covered). Add to the pan.
- In another pan, sauté the mushrooms (sliced). Add to the pan.
- Cook for about 10 minutes.
- Serve accompanied with fried bread or toast.

GOAT "CIVET" (STEWED MARINATED GOAT)

Serves: 6
Difficulty: high
Required time: 2 hours (plus time for marinating)

Ingredients:

2.5 kg goat meat
quarter litre of oil
1 litre of chicken stock
flour
salt & pepper

Marinade:

2 carrots
2 onions
2 leeks
half a litre of good red wine
stick of cinnamon
grains of black pepper
bay leaf
thyme

Method:

- In a large bowl, prepare the marinade with the goat meat (cleaned and diced in large pieces), the carrot (roughly-diced), the finely-chopped onion and leek. Add the grains of pepper, the bay leaf, the thyme and the cinnamon.
- Pour in the wine.
- Leave to marinade in a cool place for 24 hours.
- Strain well and remove the meat from the vegetables.
- Coat the meat in flour and fry until golden in hot oil, turning frequently. Remove from pan and place in an earthenware dish.
- Add the rest of the ingredients of the marinade (except the wine) to the oil and sauté.
- After about 15 minutes, add the wine and cook for approximately 15 minutes more.
- Remove pan from heat and strain the sauce. Pour the sauce over the meat in the earthenware dish. Season and cook over a low heat until the meat is tender.

QUAIL, TARRAGON-STYLE

Serves: 4
Difficulty: medium
Required time: 1 hour

Ingredients:

- *8 quails*
- *8 sweet peppers*
- *1 small onion*
- *3 ripe tomatoes*
- *150 g lard*
- *1 bouquet garni*
- *salt & pepper*

Method:

- Clean and season the quails.
- Peel and chop the onion and tomatoes.
- Melt the lard in a heatproof earthenware dish and brown the quails.
- Add the onion, tomatoes and bouquet garni. Cover with about a ladleful of water. Cover and cook over a low heat.
- Roast the peppers. Deseed and peel the peppers, taking care not to split them.
- Remove the dish from heat and take out the quails. Put one quail into each pepper.
- Strain the sauce.
- Put the stuffed peppers back into the dish and pour over the strained sauce. Cover and cook for a few minutes, adding water if necessary.

QUAIL WITH GRAPES

Serves: 4
Difficulty: low
Required time: 55 minutes

Ingredients:

- *4 quails*
- *4 slices of streaky bacon*
- *150 g fresh goose liver*
- *250 g green grapes*
- *quarter litre of milk*
- *a little chicken stock*
- *2 dl sweet Rancio wine*
- *1 lemon*
- *butter*
- *salt & pepper*

Method:

- Clean the quails well and season. Sprinkle with lemon juice.
- Stuff each one with a quarter of the liver and one grape (without skin). Wrap a slice of bacon around each quail. Secure well (by sewing or with a cocktail stick).
- Carefully sauté the quails in a little oil.
- Pour the wine into another pan and, when it has been absorbed a little, add the milk and stock. Cook until the sauce thickens.
- Peel the rest of the grapes and cook them in the butter in another pan.
- Place the quails in an ovenproof dish. Add the grapes and cover with the sauce.
- Put the dish into a preheated oven and cook for about 10 minutes.
- Serve immediately, hot.

Quail with grapes

RABBIT WITH "ALLIOLI" SAUCE

Serves:4
Difficulty: medium
Required time: 1 hour

Ingredients:

1 large rabbit
100 g lard
1 large tomato
1 carrot
1 onion
2 cloves of garlic
1 lemon
ground cinnamon
0.75 litre white wine
salt & pepper

"Allioli" sauce:

2 dl of oil
4 cloves of garlic
salt

Method:

- Rub the rabbit (cleaned and chopped in large pieces) with the lemon.
- Fry it until golden in the melted lard.
- Add the finely-chopped onion and carrot and the bay leaf.
- When they start to go brown, add the finely-chopped garlic. Stir and add the grated tomato. Sauté a little and add the wine. Cook until wine has been absorbed.
- Cook over a low heat. If necessary, add a little stock or water.
- Check seasoning.
- When the rabbit is tender, remove from the pan and place it on a serving dish.
- Serve immediately accompanied with "allioli" sauce.

Method for "allioli"sauce:

- Crush the garlic (peeled) together with the salt with a pestle and mortar. Blend into a fine paste with no lumps. Carefully add the oil little by little, stirring continuously until the sauce thickens.

Rabbit with "allioli" sauce

RABBIT IN CHOCOLATE SAUCE

Serves: 4
Difficulty: medium
Required time: 1 hour 15 minutes (plus time for marinating)

Ingredients:

1 rabbit
salt & pepper

Marinade:

half a litre of red wine
1 glass of dry sherry
1 onion
1 carrot
4 cloves of garlic
thyme
1 bay leaf
stick of cinnamon

Sauce:

4 cloves of garlic
2 pieces of vanilla-flavoured chocolate
12 almonds
pine nuts
1 glass of brandy

200 g flour
oil

Method:

- Chop the rabbit and place in a bowl. Season with salt and pepper. Finely chop all the marinade ingredients and add to the rabbit. Add the wine and sherry. Leave to marinate in a cool place for 24 hours.
- After this time, take out the rabbit pieces and dry them. Coat the pieces in flour and fry in hot oil until golden. Put the fried pieces into a heatproof earthenware dish.
- Drain the vegetables from the marinade well and sauté them in the oil used for frying the rabbit.
- When they start to turn brown, add 3 spoonfuls of flour and stir-fry a little.
- Add the wine/sherry liquid from the marinade and cook for 5 minutes.
- Strain the sauce and pour it over the rabbit. Cook, covered for about 20 minutes.
- Roast the cloves of garlic. Peel them and put them in the mortar. Crush them together with the almonds, pine nuts and chocolate. Blend well into a paste. Add the brandy.
- When well mixed, add to the rabbit and cook for 5 minutes.
- Check seasoning and serve.

"CONFITAT" (POTTED CURED PORK)

Serves: 6
Difficulty: low
Required time: 40 minutes, plus 2 days for "resting" and more time for curing.

Ingredients:

For 1 "tupí" (earthenware jar) / several glass jars:

1 whole pork loin
pork ribs
raw butifarra sausages
lard
oil
salt

Method:

- Salt the loin and ribs a little and leave to "sweat" a few days.
- Hang the butifarra sausages in a dry place and leave to cure.
- On the day of making, cut all the meat into pieces (of one helping each). Heat half the oil and half the lard, or more lard than oil. (Two kinds of fat must always be used).
- It is important to fry the meats thoroughly (if any blood is left inside, the meat could rot), but do not overcook.
- Once the meat is cooked, put it in the "tupí" or several large glass jars. When the oil is cold, add it to the "tupí"/jars.
- A layer of yellow-coloured fat will gradually form, isolating the meat from the air and thus preventing it from rotting.
- This potted pork used to be very popular and was eaten in small portions so that it would last longer.
- Metal utensils must not be used. Use only a wooden spoon.

GRILLED LAMB CHOPS WITH "ALLIOLI" SAUCE

Serves: 4
Difficulty: high
Required time: 1 hour

Ingredients:

1.5 kg lamb chops
2 dl of oil
salt

"Allioli" sauce:

1 head of garlic
3 dl of oil
salt

Method:

- Season the chops, cleaned and flattened, and coated with oil.
- Grill the chops well on both sides until well cooked.
- Serve immediately accompanied by the "allioli" sauce (served separately).

Method for "allioli" sauce:

- Crush the cloves of garlic (peeled) in a mortar with a little salt. Blend into a fine paste, with no lumps. Carefully add the oil little by little, stirring continuously until the sauce thickens.
- It is a slow, delicate process.
- In some areas of Catalonia cooked quince or apple is added, which helps to blend the mixture, without affecting the flavour of the sauce.

Suggestion:

This sauce is very important in Catalan cuisine, being used to accompany grilled meats, fish, vegetables or fish dishes.

Another way of making "allioli":

1 baked apple
1 baked potato
1 slice of toast (soaked in milk, wine or vinegar, and well-drained)
1 head of garlic
oil

- Mash the apple, potato and toast, blending well into a paste. Add the finely-chopped garlic and the oil very gradually, mixing with the pestle until a well-blended, thick sauce is made.

Grilled lamb chops with "allioli" sauce

BEEF STEW

Serves: 6
Difficulty: medium
Required time: 3 hours 20 minutes

Ingredients:

1 kg beef, shin or shoulder, etc.
150 g fresh streaky bacon
1 large onion
1 carrot
2 tomatoes
1 whole head of garlic
quarter litre of dry Rancio wine
1 small glass of liquor
2 tablesp. flour
100g lard
1 bouquet garni (bay leaf, thyme, parsley)
750 g small potatoes
500 g small onions
30 g chocolate
1 stick of cinnamon
salt & pepper

Method:

- Melt the lard in a heatproof earthenware dish. Fry the bacon.
- Roughly-dice the beef and add to the dish. Stir-fry until golden. Season with salt & pepper.
- Peel and chop the onions into medium-sized pieces, slice the carrots. Add them to the meat along with the whole head of garlic and the bouquet garni. Sauté well and then add the tomatoes (peeled and chopped). Stir. After 5 minutes, pour in the wine and liquor and add the cinnamon. Cover and cook a few minutes until the liquid has been absorbed.
- Sprinkle in the flour, and when golden, cover with hot water.
- Cook a few minutes over a high heat, then turn the heat down and cover the pan.
- Peel the potatoes and onions and boil them for 5 minutes. Drain and sauté them.
- When the meat is half-cooked, put it into another earthenware dish. Strain the sauce and pour it over the meat. Add the potatoes and onions.
- Make sure that the meat is completely covered with sauce (if necessary, add a little stock or water).
- Cook slowly until the meat is tender.
- Check seasoning.
- Serve in the same dish, garnished with chopped parsley.

Beef stew

FRICANDEAU (BRAISED VEAL)

Serves: 6
Difficulty: medium
Required time: 1 hour 30 minutes (plus 2 hours for soaking mushrooms)

Ingredients:

- *1 kg fillets of veal (top side)*
- *300 g onions*
- *2 carrots*
- *40 g dried mushrooms*
- *2 dl of olive oil*
- *1 tablesp. flour (plus flour for coating)*
- *2 dl dry white wine*
- *1 bouquet garni (bay leaf, thyme, parsley)*
- *salt & pepper*

Method:

- Soak the dried mushrooms in cold water for 2 hours. Drain well and dry.
- Season the finely-cut fillets and coat them in flour. Fry them in hot oil in a heatproof earthenware dish. Remove from dish and set aside.
- In the same oil, sauté the finely-chopped onions and carrots. Cook slowly until golden, stirring occasionally.
- Add 1 tablesp. flour and stir. When the sauce is a bit browner, add the wine. When the wine has nearly been absorbed, put the fillets back into the dish. Add a little stock or water and the bouquet garni. Cover and cook over a low heat until the meat is tender.
- 15 minutes before the meat is fully cooked, add the mushrooms.
- Check seasoning, remove the bouquet garni and serve.

Fricandeau

LAMB STEW, GIRONA-STYLE

Serves: 4
Difficulty: medium
Required time: 1 hour 15 minutes

Ingredients:

1 leg of lamb (weighing 1 kilo), chopped
150 g lard
200 g canned tomatoes
800 g mushrooms (if possible, "rovellons")
1 large onion
20 shallots
3 cloves of garlic
1 dl of oil
2 slices of bread
parsley
salt

Method:

- Put the peeled shallots in a dish with a little lard, a glass of water and salt. Place dish in a preheated moderate oven.
- Chop the leg of lamb into slices and add salt. Put in another pan with the rest of the lard and fry until golden.
- Grate the onion and add it to the lamb. Sauté and, when golden, add the tomatoes. Cover and cook over a low heat, stirring occasionally. If necessary, add a glass of water.
- Meanwhile, rinse the mushrooms several times and fry them in oil in another pan together with the slices of bread.
- Peel and chop the garlic and parsley.
- When the mushrooms and bread are fried, turn them into the pan with the lamb. Add the garlic and parsley. Cover and cook over a medium heat.
- 10 minutes before removing the pan from the heat, add the shallots and a pinch of salt.

LIVER & ONIONS

Serves: 4
Difficulty: low
Required time: 15 minutes

Ingredients:

600 g liver
600 g blood (already cooked)
100 g fresh bacon
4 onions
2 cloves of garlic
oil
pepper
finely-chopped parsley

Method:

- Peel and chop the onions finely. Fry until golden and add the chopped garlic.
- Cut the blood into pieces and add to the pan with the onions. Season and cook for 8-10 minutes.
- In another pan, fry the liver. Season.
- Turn the heat up and cook for 5 minutes.
- Mix all the ingredients in one pan, sprinkle with chopped parsley and serve.

Liver & onions

CALF'S TONGUE WITH MUSHROOM SAUCE

Serves: 4
Difficulty: medium
Required time: 1 hour 10 minutes

Ingredients:

1 calf's tongue (weighing approx. 800 g)
800 g mushrooms (if possible, "rovellons")
1 large onion
1 carrot
4 tomatoes
2.5 dl of oil and salt
1 glass of dry white wine
1 head of garlic
2 cloves
herbs
ground pepper

Method:

- Clean the tongue and cook it in boiling water for 1 minute. Take it out and scrape it with a sharp knife. Boil again for 1 minute, remove from the water and set aside.
- Peel and slice the onion and carrot and put them in an oven dish with the garlic and herbs. Put the tongue on top, season with salt and pepper and drizzle with oil. Cover and place dish in the preheated oven. Turn regularly so that it will cook evenly.
- Cut the tomatoes into halves and add them to the tongue when it is half-cooked. 5 minutes later, add the wine and, when it has been absorbed, a little water.
- Rinse and season the mushrooms. Coat them in oil and grill them.
- Serve on a separate dish.
- When the tongue is cooked, slice it and put it in another dish for serving. Strain the sauce and pour it over the tongue.

STUFFED PORK LOIN, BARCELONA-STYLE

Serves: 4
Difficulty: high
Required time: 1 hour 30 minutes (plus 2 hours for soaking prunes)

Ingredients:

8 thick pork loin fillet steaks
8 sausages
12 prunes
1 large cabbage
100 g flour
3 tomatoes
2 onions
4 small carrots
2 cloves of garlic
30 g cocoa powder
1 egg
half a glass of sparkling wine
half a glass of cream
half a glass of brandy
half a glass of white stock
1 bay leaf
thyme
1 stick of celery
salt

Method:

- A few hours before starting, soak the prunes in water. Drain well.
- Boil the cabbage, drain well and set aside with the prunes.

- Salt the fillets, slit them open lengthwise and fill each one with a sausage. Secure well with a cocktail stick. Coat in flour and fry in a little oil. Once fried, place them in a heatproof dish.
- Peel and cut the onions, garlic and 2 carrots into thin rings. Peel and grate the tomatoes.
- Sauté the onion, garlic and carrots in another pan with the bay leaf, thyme and celery. Add the tomato. When the sauce is ready, pour it into the dish with the meat. Flame it with the brandy. Pour over the sparkling wine and cream and cook until they have been absorbed. Add the stock and cook over a low heat.
- Meanwhile, beat the egg on a plate.
- Wrap the prunes in the cabbage leaves. Coat them in flour and egg. Fry them in the same oil as the meat. Remove the loin from the dish and take out the cocktail sticks. Put the loin in an earthenware dish along with the prunes.
- Strain the sauce. Dissolve the cocoa powder and add it to the sauce. Cook for 10 minutes over a low heat. Check seasoning and serve.

HARE WITH CHESTNUTS

Serves: 4
Difficulty: medium
Required time: 1 hour 30 minutes

Ingredients:

1 hare, weighing approx. 1.5 kg
100 g sausages
400 g dried chestnuts
150 g lard
350 g young shallots
1 small glass of Rancio wine
thyme
salt
grains of pepper

Method:

- Clean, chop and salt the hare.
- Peel the shallots.
- Melt the lard in a heatproof earthenware dish and fry the hare until golden. Add the shallots, the thyme and 6 grains of pepper. Stir with a wooden spoon and sauté.
- Grill the sausages. Slice them and add to the dish.
- Pour in the wine and water and cook over a low heat until the meat is tender.
- Peel and add the chestnuts when the hare is half-cooked.
- Check seasoning. Serve

PORK LOIN WITH BEANS

Serves: 4
Difficulty: low
Required time: 20 minutes

Ingredients:

- *600 g pork loin, sliced*
- *800 g cooked haricot beans*
- *2 tablesp. lard*
- *olive oil*
- *salt & pepper*

Method:

- Season the meat and fry in hot oil in a frying pan until golden on both sides. Set to one side (keep hot).
- In the same pan (with the same oil), add a little of the lard and sauté the beans.
- Stir well several times with a wooden spoon.
- When the beans turn golden brown, serve them on separate plates or a serving dish together with the pork.

PORK LOIN WITH SAUSAGES, RAISINS & PINE NUTS

Serves: 6
Difficulty: medium
Required time: 1 hour 15 minutes (plus 2 hours for soaking the raisins and pine nuts)

Ingredients:

- *1 kg pork loin (in one piece)*
- *500 g sausages*
- *200 g raisins*
- *100 g pine nuts*
- *1 onion*
- *2 tablesp. flour*
- *2 dl. of milk*
- *oil*
- *salt & pepper*
- *grated nutmeg*
- *stick of cinnamon*
- *1 dl of good white wine*

Method:

- Soak the raisins and pine nuts in warm water for about 2 hours.
- Season the loin and place it in a heatproof earthenware dish, together with the onion (cut in strips) and the cinnamon. Fry the pork until lightly browned. Add the sausages and fry. Remove them from pan and set to one side.
- Cook the pork over a low heat, and when half-cooked, pour in the wine and baste the meat several times. Leave to cook 30 minutes more. Then remove from heat and set aside to cool.
- Take out the cinnamon and add the flour. Sauté a little, stirring, and add the milk (warm). Stir well, making sure that there are no lumps. Add a little grated nutmeg. Check seasoning.
- Drain the raisins and pine nuts and add them to the sauce.
- Add the sausages.
- Cut the loin and put the slices back into the dish.
- Cook over a low heat for about 15 minutes more.
- Serve hot in the same dish.

Pork loin with beans

GOOSE WITH PEARS

Serves: 6
Difficulty: high
Required time: 1 hour 30 minutes

Ingredients:

- *1 goose (approx. 2 kg)*
- *10 firm pears*
- *50 g lard*
- *250 g onions*
- *2 carrots*
- *50 g flour*
- *water*
- *1 lemon*
- *oil*
- *thyme*
- *bay leaf*
- *salt & pepper*

Sauce:

- *50 g roasted almonds*
- *2 cloves of garlic*
- *2 plain or almond biscuits*
- *2 tablesp. vinegar*
- *parsley*

Method:

- Singe, clean and chop the goose. Season.
- Melt the lard in a heatproof earthenware dish. Add a little oil.
- When the oil is hot, fry the goose until golden. Set to one side.
- In the same fat (after having poured a little out), sauté the finely-chopped onions and carrots. Add the flour and cook slowly until brown.
- Add enough water to barely cover the goose meat and bring to the boil. Add the meat, cover and simmer for about 45 minutes.
- Add the thyme.
- Meanwhile, peel the pears, rub them with lemon and boil, whole, for about 3 minutes. Remove them from the pan and leave them to cool.
- Coat them in flour and fry until golden in a little oil or fat used to cook the goose.
- Crush the garlic, parsley, almonds and biscuits with a pestle and mortar.
- Once they have been finely crushed, add the vinegar and blend well. Add a little of the sauce from the dish.
- When the goose is half-cooked, add the almond mixture. Stir well and place earthenware dish in a preheated oven (180°C).
- When the goose is nearly cooked, add the pears (well-drained).
- Finish cooking.
- Check seasoning. Serve hot in the same dish.

Goose with pears

PIG'S EAR, MARESME-STYLE

Serves: 4
Difficulty: high
Required time: 2 hours

Ingredients:

- *6 pig's ears*
- *200 g flour*
- *70 g butter*
- *half an onion*
- *2.5 dl of oil*
- *1 litre of milk*
- *1 bay leaf*
- *1 thyme sprig*
- *stick of cinnamon and ground cinnamon*
- *grains of pepper*
- *salt*

Method:

- Slightly singe the pig's ears and scrape them with a sharp knife under a cold tap. Rinse well.
- Put the ears into a pan with cold water. Bring to the boil and blanch them. Discard this water and fill the pan again, adding the thyme, the bay leaf, the cinnamon stick, the chopped onion, salt and pepper. Bring to the boil and cook until the ears are soft.
- Meanwhile, prepare the sauce. Heat the milk in a pan and set to one side. Melt the butter in a frying pan over a low heat and add the flour gradually, stirring continuously with a wooden spoon. Pour the milk in gradually, until you have a not-too-thick white sauce.
- Add the ears to the sauce and cook for 10 minutes.
- Before serving, sprinkle with salt and ground cinnamon.

ROAST DUCK, BARCELONA-STYLE

Serves: 4
Difficulty: low
Required time: 40 minutes

Ingredients:

- *2 ducks weighing 1 kg each*
- *150 g lard*
- *1 small onion*
- *half a head of garlic*
- *1 bouquet garni (bay leaf, oregano, cloves, thyme and a little piece of carrot)*
- *half a glass of brandy*
- *half a glass of Rancio wine*
- *hazelnuts, almonds and pine nuts*
- *salt & pepper*

Method:

- Chop and season the duck. Fry it in the lard until golden. Cover and cook over a low heat.
- Peel and finely-slice the onion into rings as well as the garlic. Sauté them with the bouquet garni in the pan. Stir a little and add the wine and brandy.
- Meanwhile, crush a handful of almonds, hazelnuts and pine nuts. Blend with a little water and add to the pan.
- Simmer gently until the sauce is ready and the duck is tender.

Roast duck, Barcelona-style

STUFFED TURKEY

Serves: 6-8
Difficulty: high
Required time: 3 hours 30 minutes

Ingredients:

- *1 turkey, weighing approx. 2.5 kg*
- *200 g pork loin*
- *150 g sausages*
- *100 g prunes*
- *50 g dried peaches/apricots*
- *50 g raisins*
- *30 g pine nuts*
- *150 g lard*
- *half a litre of Rancio wine*
- *ground cinnamon*
- *salt & pepper*

Method:

- Singe and clean the turkey well inside and outside, removing tendons from legs and the breastbone. Keep the liver. Make sure you leave enough skin on the neck so that you can bend it.
- Season the turkey inside with salt, pepper, ground cinnamon and a little wine.
- Soak the prunes, raisins, dried peaches and pine nuts for a while in warm water.
- Melt a little lard and fry the pork loin (chopped), sausages and turkey liver.
- When they start to turn golden, add the prunes (stoned), raisins, dried peaches and pine nuts (well-drained). Add a little pepper and ground cinnamon and stir with a wooden spoon.
- Pour in a little wine. Set aside to cool.
- When the mixture is ready, stuff the turkey with it, sewing it up well with butcher's string.
- Tie the legs and wings tightly and make sure that the breast is well-stuffed and well-presented.
- Grease the whole turkey with lard and sprinkle with salt. Cover with untrimmed paper and put in an oven dish. Cover.
- Roast slowly in a low, preheated, oven, basting it every now and then.
- After about 1 hour and 15 minutes, remove the paper so that the turkey will be browned. Drizzle with the rest of the wine and a little stock.
- Continue roasting (basting frequently) until completely cooked.
- Take the turkey out of the dish, remove the grease from the gravy and strain the latter.
- Before serving, cut and discard the string. If the turkey is to be carved at the table, place it on a hot serving dish garnished with cress.
- If you prefer to carve it in the kitchen, cut it in half lengthwise, take out the stuffing and transfer it to a dish. On top of the stuffing, arrange the legs (cut in three) and the breast (carved in slices). Drizzle with a little of the sauce and place in the oven to keep it warm before serving.
- Garnish with cress.
- Serve accompanied with the rest of the sauce and a green salad.

PARTRIDGE A LA VINAIGRETTE

Serves: 4
Difficulty: medium
Required time: 2 hours 15 minutes

Ingredients:

4 partridges
8 onions
1 head of garlic
salt
bay leaves
pepper
lemon juice
half a litre of oil
half a litre of sherry vinegar

Method:

- Clean the partridges well and chop them in two lengthwise. Sprinkle with lemon juice and season with salt and pepper.
- Sauté the partridges in a little oil and remove from heat before they start turning brown.
- Put clean oil in an earthenware dish. Add a little of the vinegar, the onions (cut in pieces), the head of garlic and several bayleaves. Add the partridges. Cover and cook over a low heat until tender (approximately 2 hours).
- A little before the partridges are fully cooked, add the rest of the vinegar and check seasoning.
- Serve one partridge in the centre of each plate, surrounded by the onions. Pour over the vinegar sauce.

PIG'S TROTTERS WITH MALMSEY

Serves: 6
Difficulty: medium
Required time: 1 hour 30 minutes

Ingredients:

6 pig's trotters
1 onion
1 leek
1 carrot
celery
3 cloves of garlic
1 dl of oil
2.5 dl malmsey
4 cloves
1 bay leaf
sprig of thyme
salt
grains of pepper

Method:

- Clean the pig's trotters and cut in two lengthwise. Put them in a pan with water and bring quickly to the boil. Discard this water and put clean water in the pan (enough to cover the trotters).
- Leave to cook for a while.
- Meanwhile, chop the celery, carrot, garlic and leek. Halve the onion and stick in the cloves. Add them all to the same pan as the trotters, together with the bay leaf, the thyme and a few grains of pepper. Pour in the oil and cook until the trotters are half tender.
- Heat the malmsey in a saucepan and add a little of the stock from the pig's trotters.
- Pour into the pan with the other ingredients and cook until the trotters are tender and the stock thickens into a sauce.

Pork loin with beans

GOOSE WITH PEARS

Serves: 6
Difficulty: high
Required time: 1 hour 30 minutes

Ingredients:

1 goose (approx. 2 kg)
10 firm pears
50 g lard
250 g onions
2 carrots
50 g flour
water
1 lemon
oil
thyme
bay leaf
salt & pepper

Sauce:

50 g roasted almonds
2 cloves of garlic
2 plain or almond biscuits
2 tablesp. vinegar
parsley

Method:

- Singe, clean and chop the goose. Season.
- Melt the lard in a heatproof earthenware dish. Add a little oil.
- When the oil is hot, fry the goose until golden. Set to one side.
- In the same fat (after having poured a little out), sauté the finely-chopped onions and carrots. Add the flour and cook slowly until brown.
- Add enough water to barely cover the goose meat and bring to the boil. Add the meat, cover and simmer for about 45 minutes.
- Add the thyme.
- Meanwhile, peel the pears, rub them with lemon and boil, whole, for about 3 minutes. Remove them from the pan and leave them to cool.
- Coat them in flour and fry until golden in a little oil or fat used to cook the goose.
- Crush the garlic, parsley, almonds and biscuits with a pestle and mortar.
- Once they have been finely crushed, add the vinegar and blend well. Add a little of the sauce from the dish.
- When the goose is half-cooked, add the almond mixture. Stir well and place earthenware dish in a preheated oven (180°C).
- When the goose is nearly cooked, add the pears (well-drained).
- Finish cooking.
- Check seasoning. Serve hot in the same dish.

Goose with pears

PIG'S EAR, MARESME-STYLE

Serves: 4
Difficulty: high
Required time: 2 hours

Ingredients:

6 pig's ears
200 g flour
70 g butter
half an onion
2.5 dl of oil
1 litre of milk
1 bay leaf
1 thyme sprig
stick of cinnamon and ground cinnamon
grains of pepper
salt

Method:

- Slightly singe the pig's ears and scrape them with a sharp knife under a cold tap. Rinse well.
- Put the ears into a pan with cold water. Bring to the boil and blanch them. Discard this water and fill the pan again, adding the thyme, the bay leaf, the cinnamon stick, the chopped onion, salt and pepper. Bring to the boil and cook until the ears are soft.
- Meanwhile, prepare the sauce. Heat the milk in a pan and set to one side. Melt the butter in a frying pan over a low heat and add the flour gradually, stirring continuously with a wooden spoon. Pour the milk in gradually, until you have a not-too-thick white sauce.
- Add the ears to the sauce and cook for 10 minutes.
- Before serving, sprinkle with salt and ground cinnamon.

ROAST DUCK, BARCELONA-STYLE

Serves: 4
Difficulty: low
Required time: 40 minutes

Ingredients:

2 ducks weighing 1 kg each
150 g lard
1 small onion
half a head of garlic
1 bouquet garni (bay leaf, oregano, cloves, thyme and a little piece of carrot)
half a glass of brandy
half a glass of Rancio wine
hazelnuts, almonds and pine nuts
salt & pepper

Method:

- Chop and season the duck. Fry it in the lard until golden. Cover and cook over a low heat.
- Peel and finely-slice the onion into rings as well as the garlic. Sauté them with the bouquet garni in the pan. Stir a little and add the wine and brandy.
- Meanwhile, crush a handful of almonds, hazelnuts and pine nuts. Blend with a little water and add to the pan.
- Simmer gently until the sauce is ready and the duck is tender.

The most typical of all dessert is surely "crema catalana"; however, each festivity has its corresponding sweet or pastry: for example, "coca de Sant Joan" (Midsummer's day), "panellets on All Saints' day, or "turrón" at Christmas time, and not to mention many specialities of home baking for which Catalonia is well-renowned.

"Buñuelos", Ampurdán-style (Anise-flavoured fried doughnuts)

Makes: 40
Difficulty: medium
Required time: 2 hours

Ingredients:

- *350 g flour*
- *50 g butter*
- *20 g baker's yeast*
- *60 g sugar*
- *half a dl of milk*
- *rind of lemon*
- *3 medium-sized eggs*
- *a pinch of salt*
- *half a glass of anisette*
- *1 teasp. ground aniseed*
- *half a teasp. ground coriander*
- *ground cinnamon*
- *oil for frying*
- *sugar for dusting*

Method:

- Warm the milk and blend it with the yeast and 100 g flour. Work into a ball.
- Cover with a clean cloth and prove in a warm place for 30 minutes.
- Sift the remaining flour and add the softened butter, the eggs, salt, sugar, anisette and all the spices. Mix well with a fork and add the proved dough.
- Knead into a soft dough.
- Turn it onto a floured board and knock it back.
- Grease the board and your hands with oil and scoop off pieces of dough. Shape each piece into a ball and place them on a greased baking sheet.
- Leave to rise in a warm place. The dough has to double in bulk. (Approximately 1 hour).
- Heat oil in a deep frying pan. Make a hole in the centre of each ball and fry them until golden. (Make sure that the oil is not too hot, as they burn easily).
- Dust with sugar.

Pig's trotters with malmsey

PIG'S TROTTERS WITH PARSNIPS

Serves: 4
Difficulty: high
Required time: 2 hours 25 minutes

Ingredients:

4 pig's trotters (not too big)
500 g parsnips
2 dl of oil
2 tablesp. of breadcrumbs
flour

Stock:

water
1 bay leaf
salt
2 dl of white wine
1 clove
1 onion
parsley
oregano
1 carrot
grains of pepper

Sauce 1:

oil or lard
1 onion
2 cloves of garlic
2 ripe tomatoes
half a dl of Rancio wine

Sauce 2:

25 g roasted almonds
parsley
1 clove of garlic
2 sweet biscuits
Rancio wine

Method:

- Singe the pig's trotters, scrape them with a sharp knife. Wash and dry.
- Chop them in half lengthwise and tie the halves together again with butcher's string so that they won't lose their shape when cooking.
- Put them into a pan with all the stock ingredients, making sure that they are well covered by the water. Remove foam from the top as soon as the water begins to boil.
- Cover and simmer for about 2 hours.
- When ready, remove from pan and set to one side.
- Make sauce 1. Heat the oil or lard in a heatproof earthenware dish and sauté the finely-chopped onion until golden.
- Add the chopped garlic and tomatoes (crushed) and cook for a few minutes. Pour in the wine and cook until it has been absorbed a little.
- Add the trotters and cook for about 15 minutes.
- Make sauce 2. Crush all the dry ingredients with a pestle and mortar, mix well and blend with a little wine. Add to the earthenware dish and cover with some of the water from cooking the trotters.
- Peel and chop the parsnips. Boil in salted water for 25 minutes.
- When the parsnips are cooked, drain well. Coat in flour and fry in hot oil. Add them to the earthenware dish. Cook for 10 minutes.
- Check seasoning.
- Place dish, covered, in preheated oven (200°C) for about 15 minutes.
- Remove from oven and sprinkle with breadcrumbs. Return to oven and grill.
- Serve in the same dish.

PIG'S TROTTERS, STUFFED

Serves: 4
Difficulty: high
Required time: 2 hours 30 minutes

Ingredients:

4 pig's trotters

Stuffing:

400 g minced pork
2 eggs
200 g mushrooms
10 g truffles
1 glass of malmsey
half a glass of anisette

Sauce:

lard
1 onion
3 medium-sized tomatoes
2 cloves of garlic
2 cloves
flour
half a litre of dry white wine
20 figs
salt & pepper

Method:

- Singe the pig's trotters, scrape them with a sharp knife. Wash and dry. Cover them with water and cook until tender. Leave to cool. Remove the bone. Set to one side. (Keep some of the stock made when cooking them).
- Make the stuffing by mixing all its ingredients evenly and season with salt.
- Fill the trotters with this mixture and sew them up. Sauté them in a little lard. Set to one side.
- Put the rest of the lard into an ovenproof earthenware dish. Peel and chop the onion, the tomatoes and the garlic. Fry them in the lard, adding the cloves and a little pepper. Sprinkle with a little flour. Place the dish a few minutes in the oven (preheated) until the flour browns. Add the wine and cook in oven until the wine has been absorbed. Add the stuffed pig's trotters and cover them with the stock reserved. Cook for a further 30 minutes.
- Meanwhile, boil the figs. When ready, drain and set to one side.
- Take the trotters out of the dish. Strain the sauce. Return the trotters to the dish along with the figs. Cover with the sauce. Bring to the boil over a low heat.
- Serve in another dish.

CHICKEN & LOBSTER

Serves: 4
Difficulty: high
Required time: 1 hour 10 minutes

Ingredients:

1 chicken (weighing approx. 1.5 kg)
2 lobsters (weighing 750 g each)
3 dl of olive oil
50 g lard
1 large onion
3 tomatoes
50 g flour
1 bouquet garni (thyme, oregano, parsley)
1 bay leaf
a little leek
1 glass liquor
quarter litre of dry Rancio wine
a little chicken stock
a few slices of bread
salt & pepper
ground cinnamon
oil

Sauce:

50 g roasted almonds and hazelnuts
40 g grated chocolate
2 cloves of garlic
saffron
parsley
salt & pepper

Garnish:

8 slices of toast

Method:

- Chop the chicken into equal-sized pieces. Season and sprinkle with cinnamon.
- Heat the lard and a little oil in a heatproof earthenware dish and add the chicken pieces. Cover and fry quickly.
- When it starts to turn golden, turn the heat down a little and add the sliced onion. Stir-fry until it starts going brown. Add the chopped tomatoes and sauté until the juice has evaporated a little. Add the wine and liquor and cook until they have been absorbed.
- Sprinkle over flour and drizzle with stock or water, enough to barely cover the chicken. Add the bouquet garni. Cover and cook very gently.
- Remove the legs from the lobsters. Set to one side.
- Cut the lobsters into 6 pieces, from top to bottom and cut in half lengthwise. Remove and discard the stomach, but keep the liver.
- Also reserve the blood.
- Season the chopped lobster pieces and add them to the dish with the chicken.
- Make the sauce, using a pestle and mortar. Crush the almonds, hazelnuts, garlic, parsley, lobster liver and grated chocolate. Add a little ground pepper, salt and saffron. Mix well into a fine paste with the pestle. Add the blood and a little of the sauce from the dish.
- Pour the mixture into the dish and cook until ready. Make sure there is not too much sauce. Check seasoning.
- Strain the sauce. Transfer the chicken and lobster to another earthenware dish. Pour over the sauce.
- Garnish with triangles of toast.

Chicken & lobster

STUFFED CHICKEN

Serves: 8
Difficulty: high
Required time: 2 hours

Ingredients:

1 chicken (approx. 3 kg)
50 g lard
salt oil

Stuffing:

1 can of truffles
2 eggs
300 g minced pork
1 medium-sized Golden Delicious apple
35 g ham
25 g pine nuts
12 dried apricots
12 prunes
25 g raisins
1 chicken liver
1 glass of brandy

Sauce:

1 onion
1 medium-sized carrot
quarter litre of dry white wine
quarter litre of chicken stock
half a stick of cinnamon
1 bouquet garni (bay leaf, thyme, parsley)
oil
salt & pepper

Method:

- Clean and singe the chicken. Season and set to one side.
- Stone the prunes (and raisins if necessary) and chop. Cut up the dried apricots. Peel and dice the apple.
- Turn the fruit into a large bowl and mix with the mince, the truffle, the diced ham and liver.
- Add the beaten eggs, then the pine nuts and the brandy. Mix well with a wooden spoon and season.
- Fill the chicken with this stuffing and sew up.
- Place the chicken in an ovenproof earthenware dish. Season it on both sides. Add the onion, carrot, bouquet garni and cinnamon stick. Grease the chicken with lard and oil.
- Place in a preheated oven (210°C) and cook for 30 minutes. Turn and cook for a further 30 minutes. Pour over the wine and stock.
- Lower the oven temperature and cook for about 20 minutes more, basting frequently.
- Serve hot.

Stuffed chicken

STEWED VEAL & MUSHROOMS

Serves: 4
Difficulty: medium
Required time: 1 hour 15 minutes

Ingredients:

1.200 kg veal (hind knuckle)
800 g mushrooms (if possible, "rovellons")
1 onion
1 carrot
4 ripe tomatoes
150 g flour
50 g lard
2 dl of oil
salt
1 bay leaf
grains of pepper
3 cloves
1 dl of liquor

Method:

- Cut the meat into fillets of about 40 g. Season and coat in flour.
- Fry in melted lard and hot oil.
- When golden, remove from pan and set aside.
- Pour the grease from the pan into a heatproof earthenware dish and sauté the finely-sliced carrot and onion. Add the bay leaf.
- Fry lightly for a few minutes and then add the diced tomatoes.
- When the tomatoes are well cooked, season and add the cloves. Add the liquor and cover with hot water.
- Simmer for a few minutes and then add the meat. Cook over a low heat.
- When the meat is nearly cooked, remove the dish from the heat.
- Take the meat out and strain the sauce. Return the meat to the dish and pour over the sauce.
- Wash the mushrooms well. Chop and sauté a little in hot oil.
- Add the mushrooms to the meat and sauce in the dish.
- Cook for about 10 minutes.
- Check seasoning.
- Serve hot.

Stewed veal & mushrooms

DESSERTS & SWEETS

"Buñuelos", Ampurdán-style

"BUÑUELOS", VENDRELL-STYLE
(RICH HAZELNUT PASTRIES)

Serves: 10
Difficulty: low
Required time: 50 minutes

Ingredients:

- *1 kg flour*
- *3 kg icing sugar*
- *1.200 kg roasted hazelnuts*
- *200 g bicarbonate of soda*
- *12 eggs*

Method:

- Crush the hazelnuts well with a pestle and mortar.
- In a large bowl, mix the icing sugar, the crushed hazelnuts and the whites of 10 eggs. Gradually add the flour and bicarbonate of soda and mix well into a stiff dough.
- Heat the oven at 180ºC.
- Roll out the dough and cut into squares.
- Place the squares on a greased baking sheet.
- Brush the top of the squares with the other 2 eggs (beaten).
- Bake in the oven until golden. Leave to cool.

"CARQUINYOLIS"
(HARD ALMOND BISCUITS)

Serves: 6
Difficulty: low
Required time: 50 minutes

Ingredients:

- *100 g raw almonds*
- *2 eggs*
- *rind of 1 lemon*
- *100 g sugar*
- *175 g flour*
- *1 teasp. baking powder*
- *half a teasp. ground cinnamon*
- *a few drops of anisette*

Method:

- Sift the flour and baking powder. Make a well in the centre and add 1 egg, the sugar, the lemon rind and the cinnamon. Mix a little and add the whole almonds. Flavour with the anisette.
- Mix and knead well into a stiff dough. Shape the dough into rolls of approximately 3 cm long and half as thick. Place the rolls on a greased baking sheet.
- Brush with a little beaten egg yolk mixed with a few drops of water.
- Bake in a preheated low oven until they start to turn a golden colour.
- Remove tray from oven and, whilst still hot, cut each roll diagonally in two, (if this is done when cold, they will break).
- Return the biscuits to the oven and finish baking.

"Carquinyolis"

"COCA" PASTRIES

Serves: 4
Difficulty: low
Required time: 1 hour

Ingredients:

- *800 g flour*
- *400 g sugar*
- *400 g lard*
- *4 eggs*
- *1 lemon*

Method:

- Put the lard, the sugar, the egg yolks and the grated lemon rind into a large bowl. Mix well and sift in the flour gradually. Blend well until thick.
- Turn the dough onto a floured board and roll to a maximum thickness of 2 cm.
- Using different-shaped cutters, cut the dough into several pieces. Place them on a greased baking tray.
- Bake in a moderate oven until golden.

"COCA DE SANT JOAN" (FRUITED YEAST BREAD)

Serves: 6
Difficulty: medium
Required time: 1 hour 25 minutes

Ingredients:

- *2 dl of warm milk*
- *300 g flour*
- *50 g butter*
- *30 g baker's yeast*
- *rind of 1 lemon*
- *1 egg*
- *150 g glacé cherries and candied fruit (melon)*
- *50 g pine nuts*

Almond paste:

- *200 g ground almonds*
- *200 g icing sugar*
- *1.25 dl of milk*

Method:

- Mix the yeast with the warm milk.
- Mix it with the butter, the grated lemon rind and 200 g of flour. Knead well and add the rest of the flour. Shape the dough into a smooth and elastic ball.
- Turn onto a lightly floured board and work the sugar carefully into the dough.
- Grease a baking sheet with butter and spread out the dough, flattening it equally and pinch the edges.
- Cover and leave at room temperature until doubled in bulk.
- When it has risen, glaze with the almond paste* and decorate with the candied fruit and pine nuts.

- Bake in a preheated moderate-hot oven for 30 minutes.

***Almond paste:**

- Carefully mix the milk and icing sugar. Add the ground almonds. Blend well into a light paste (to a glazing consistency).

"CREMA CATALANA" (BAKED CUSTARD WITH CARAMELISED TOPPING)

Serves: 4-5
Difficulty: medium
Required time: 30 minutes

Ingredients:

half a dl of milk
4 egg yolks
125 g sugar
20 g cornflour
stick of cinnamon
rind of 1 lemon
40 g sugar for making caramelised topping

Method:

- Wash and brush the lemon. Cut the lemon rind carefully (only the yellow part)
- Dissolve the cornflour in a little milk.
- Pour the rest of the milk into a saucepan. Add the lemon rind and cinnamon stick. Bring to the boil and remove pan from heat.
- In another saucepan, beat the egg yolks and sugar together. Beat into a creamy consistency.
- Stir the warm milk into this mixture with a hand whisk.
- Strain the dissolved cornflour and add it to the milk and eggs. Stir continuously until the custard thickens, but don't let it boil.
- As soon as the custard thickens, remove the pan from the heat and beat the custard well (to prevent it from curdling).
- Pour into a bowl (or individual ones).
- Leave to cool at room temperature.
- When completely cool, and, just before serving, sprinkle with sugar. Caramelise the sugar by burning it with a special hot rod, thus making the caramelised topping.

ORANGE CRÈME CARAMEL

Serves: 6
Difficulty: low
Required time: 1 hour 10 minutes

Ingredients:

6 sweet oranges
6 eggs
200 g sugar

Method:

- Squeeze the oranges.
- Separate the egg yolks from the whites. Mix the yolks with the sugar and orange juice.
- Pour into a mould. Place the mould in another container with hot/boiling water and cook until completely set.

DRESSED STRAWBERRIES

Serves: 6
Difficulty: low
Required time: 15 minutes

Ingredients:

1 kg strawberries
2 tablesp. vinegar
150 g sugar

Method:

- Rinse the strawberries carefully in cold water. Hull them. If large, cut in half; if small, leave whole.
- Put the strawberries into a glass or china bowl/dish. Add the vinegar and sugar. Stir carefully in order not to bruise them. Leave in a cool place for at least 2 hours.
- Best served with whipped cream.

CARAMELISED NUTS

Serves: 6
Difficulty: low
Required time: 20 minutes

Ingredients:

100 g roasted almonds
100 g roasted hazelnuts
100 g walnuts
400 g sugar
a little water

Method:

- Make a caramel syrup by dissolving the sugar in the water. Stir with a wooden spoon, making sure that the syrup doesn't stick to the bottom.
- When it thickens to a brown, caramel syrup, add the nuts. Stir.
- Stir continuously for a few minutes. Make sure that all the nuts get equally coated and that they don't stick to the bottom.
- Grease a deep tray or board with oil. Turn the caramelised nuts onto the tray and separate them with a spatula. Leave to cool.
- Best kept in a glass jar.

Dressed strawberries

BAKED APPLES

Serves: 4
Difficulty: low
Required time: 35 minutes

Ingredients:

4 Golden Delicious apples
1 glass of white wine
3 drops of sweetener

Method:

- Wash and core the apples and place them in an oven dish.
- Mix the sweetener with the wine and put a spoonful into the centre of each apple.
- Pour the rest of the wine over the apples.
- Bake in a moderate oven for about 30 minutes, basting occasionally.
- Allow to cool before serving.

"MEL I MATÓ" (COTTAGE CHEESE WITH HONEY)

Serves: 4
Difficulty: low
Required time: 30 minutes

Ingredients:

1 litre of goat's or cow's milk
10 g powdered rennet
2 dl of water
honey

Method:

- Dissolve the rennet in the water.
- Put the milk in a pan and bring to boil.
- Add 4 tablesp. of the rennet mixture and stir.
- Immediately, strain the milk carefully into a bowl, using a *very fine* sieve.
- Make sure that the whey is well separated from the curd - the curd, or "mató", being left in the sieve.
- This "mató" can be eaten with sugar or chopped almonds, but the best way to do so is with honey.
- Divide the curd into 4 portions and serve drizzled with honey.

"Mel i mató"

"MANJAR BLANC" (ALMOND MILK PUDDING)

Serves: 6
Difficulty: medium
Required time: 45 minutes

Ingredients:

400 g sweet almonds
200 g sugar
50 g cornflour
5 bitter almonds
rind of 1 lemon
1 stick of cinnamon
almond oil
salt
water

Method:

- Peel the almonds and crush them with a pestle and mortar. Add a little water, and blend to a fine paste.
- Mix the paste with 1 litre of water and strain (with a muslin cloth) to obtain the almond milk. Keep 4 or 5 spoonfuls in the fridge.
- Pour the rest of the almond milk into a saucepan together with the lemon rind, sugar, a pinch of salt and the cinnamon stick.
- In another saucepan, mix the cornflour with the rest of the cold almond milk, then add it to the other pan, mixing well.
- Bring to the boil and stir continuously with a wooden spoon. Remove from heat.
- Pour into a mould greased with almond oil.
- Leave to cool before serving.

BLACKBERRY JAM

Serves: 6
Difficulty: low
Required time: 40 minutes, (plus 12 hours for maceration)

Ingredients:

1 kg wild ripe blackberries
750 g sugar
1 glass of water
juice of 1 lemon

Method:

- Wash the blackberries gently in a colander, taking care not to bruise the fruit. Strain and weigh.
- Put the fruit in a pan and add 750 g sugar per kilo. Sprinkle with lemon juice and add 1 glass of water.
- After 12 hours, cook gently in the same pan for about 25 minutes (until the fruit is soft).
- Meanwhile, wash a few jars thoroughly (or sterilise them by boiling them for 10 minutes) and then leave to dry, upside-down, on a very clean cloth.
- After 25 minutes, whisk the jam slightly. Return to heat and bring to the boil. Cook for a further 5 minutes, stirring continuously.
- Pot jam at once and cover. Turn the jars upside-down and leave until completely cold.
- When the jam is cold, turn the jars upright, label them and store in a dark, cool place.

CANDIED FRUIT & SUGARED YOLK "MONA" (EASTER CAKE)

Serves: 8
Difficulty: high
Required time: 1 hour 15 minutes

Ingredients:

Cake:

6 large eggs
180 g sugar
130 g flour
rind of 1 lemon
50 g ground almonds
1 teasp. baking powder

Filling:

200 g apricot jam
5 tablesp. sugar
lemon juice
liquor or sweet wine

Sugared yolk:

3 egg yolks
sugar (the same weight as the yolks)

Decoration:

candied fruits
chocolate eggs
apple jelly
feathers
coloured sweets
chopped almonds

Method:

- Whisk the eggs, sugar. And the grated lemon rind until doubled in bulk.
- Carefully sift in the flour and the baking powder. Add the ground almonds carefully.
- Turn into a greased 30 cm mould. Cook in a preheated oven at 180°C for about 30 minutes.
- Turn out to cool on a wire tray.
- When cold, slice the cake across in two. Sprinkle the bottom layer with a little liquor/sweet wine and spread with jam, mixed with sugar and lemon juice. Re-assemble the cake. Spread the sugared yolk* over the top layer. Arrange the candied fruits. Brush with apple jelly (warm).
- Brush the sides of the cake with warm apple jelly and coat with chopped almonds.
- Decorate with chocolate eggs and feathers.
- Serve on a doyley on a tray.

*Sugared yolk:

- Beat the egg yolks and sugar well.
- Heat in a saucepan, stirring continuously with a wooden spatula/spoon.
- When the mixture starts to thicken and to stick to the spatula/spoon, remove pan from heat.
- Keep on stirring and return to the heat.
- Before it reaches boiling point, remove from heat again and beat well.
- Turn onto a tray and leave to cool.
- Use when cold.

"ORELLETES" (SWEET FRITTERS)

Serves: 4
Difficulty: low
Required time: 40 minutes

Ingredients:

500 g flour
150 g sugar
3 eggs
half a small cup of oil
1 glass of anisette
half a glass of muscatel
vanilla essence
rind of 1 lemon
salt
oil for frying

Method:

- Sift the flour into a large bowl. Make a well in the centre and add the eggs, sugar, oil, anisette, muscatel, a few drops of vanilla essence, grated rind and a pinch of salt.
- Knead well into a soft and elastic dough. Don't overknead. Make into a ball.
- Scoop off pieces of dough weighing about 25 g each. Shape each piece into balls. Cover and leave to prove in a warm place for about 25 minutes.
- When the dough is ready, roll each ball out into a flat round.
- Shape each round by twisting and overlapping and fry in hot oil. When golden, turn and fry on the other side.
- Drain well. Serve coated with sugar.

"Orelletes"

"PANELLETS" (ALMOND CAKES)

Serves: 8-10
Difficulty: medium
Required time: 1 hour 15 minutes

Ingredients:

Dough:

500 g ground almonds
500 g sugar
150 g potatoes
rind of 1 lemon

Decoration:

100 g pine nuts
100 g raw chopped almonds
100 g desiccated coconut
25 g cocoa powder
2 eggs
cornflour

Method:

- Boil the potatoes with skin. Peel and mash. Set aside to cool.
- Mix the potatoes with the ground almonds. Add the sugar gradually in small quantities. Mix well with a wooden spatula/spoon. Add the grated lemon rind and mix with fingers.
- Divide the dough into portions, depending on what kinds of "panellets"* are going to be made.

*Pine nut:

- Make little balls. Coat with cornflour, beaten egg white and pine nuts. Brush with beaten egg yolk.

*Almond:

- Make strips. Shape into crescents. Coat with cornflour, beaten egg white and chopped almonds. Brush with beaten egg yolk.

*Coconut:

- Add the coconut to the basic almond mixture. Make into pyramid shapes and coat with desiccated coconut. Brush the tip with beaten egg yolk.

*Chocolate:

- Mix 25 g cocoa powder into the almond dough. Make little balls. Coat with egg white and sugar.
- Place all cakes on baking trays greased with butter.
- Bake in preheated oven at 220°C for 10-12 minutes.
- When cool, arrange on a tray with a doyley.

TORTOSA "PATISSETS" (PUMPKIN CAKES)

Serves: 6
Difficulty: medium
Required time: 1 hour 45 minutes

Ingredients:

Filling:

1 pumpkin
1 lemon
a stick of cinnamon
800 g sugar

Pastry:

200 g sugar
1 large egg
2 dl of good liquor
3 and a quarter dl of oil
800 g (approx.) flour
salt

Method:

Filling:

- Cut, clean and peel the pumpkin, removing all seeds. Cover with cold water.
- Put the pumpkin in a pan with water and cook for about 25 minutes. Drain well and weigh out the exact amount required.
- Put required amount of pumpkin into a saucepan with the lemon juice and rind, the cinnamon stick and sugar (800 g per each kg of pumpkin). Cook, uncovered, for about 45 minutes until thick.
- Set aside to cool.

Pastry:

- Meanwhile, prepare the pastry.
- In a bowl, beat the egg and sugar with a wooden spatula/spoon. Add the liquor, oil and, finally, sift in the flour. Mix well and then turn onto a floured board. Work into a soft ball of dough.
- Divide the dough into little balls. Work each ball until soft and elastic.
- Make into rounds and flatten.
- Place a little of the pumpkin filling in the centre of each round. Damp the edges of the pastry and draw them together over the filling. Pinch firmly together.
- Bake in a preheated oven at 200°C for about 20 minutes until golden brown.
- When ready, sprinkle with sugar.

PEARS WITH SHERRY CARAMEL SAUCE

Serves: 4
Difficulty: medium
Required time: 30 minutes

Ingredients:

1 can of pears in syrup
150 g sugar
1 tablesp. cornflour
1 glass of sweet sherry

Method:

- Drain the pears and arrange in a dish. Set aside.
- Put the sugar and 1 spoonful of the syrup in a pan. Boil to a caramel consistency and colour.
- In another pan, heat the rest of the syrup and then add it to the caramel.
- Dissolve the cornflour in the sherry and mix in with the caramel.
- Blend the sauce well and pour over the pears.
- Serve.

PEARS WITH EGG CUSTARD (COOKED IN MILK AND TOPPED WITH MERINGUE)

Serves: 6-7
Difficulty: medium
Required time: 45 minutes

Ingredients:

2 litres of milk
14 pears
300 g sugar
a stick of cinnamon
8 eggs

Method:

- Peel the pears. Put them in a saucepan with the milk, sugar and cinnamon stick.
- Boil for 20 minutes, making sure the milk does not boil over.
- Take out the pears and drain. Leave to cool on a tray.
- Separate all the egg whites and yolks. Beat the yolks and stir them gradually into the milk until the custard thickens.
- Pour the custard over the pears.
- Whisk the egg whites until stiff. Add a little sugar and top the pears with the meringue.
- Leave to cool in the fridge before serving.
- May be decorated with glacé cherries or pears.

Pears with custard

BAKED PEARS, CATALAN-STYLE

Serves: 6
Difficulty: low
Required time: 1 hour 15 minutes (plus 1 hour for macerating)

Ingredients:

12 bananas
100 g roasted hazelnuts
50 g sugar
1 dl of brandy
ground cinnamon
butter for greasing oven tray

Method:

- Slit the banana skins lengthwise in order to remove the banana without spoiling the skin, which will be used to serve the dessert.
- Slice the bananas and put them into a large bowl. Add the sugar, the roughly-chopped hazelnuts and the brandy.
- Leave to macerate 1 hour.
- Fill the banana skins with this mixture (without the brandy).
- Grease an oven tray with the butter. Place the bananas on the tray.
- Cook in a preheated oven for 15 minutes.
- Flame with the brandy left over from the maceration and serve at the table.

PEACHES WITH EGG CUSTARD

Serves: 4
Difficulty: low
Required time: 20 minutes

Ingredients:

1 can of peaches in syrup
2 eggs
1 small glass of milk
3 teasp. of sugar
3 teasp. of desiccated coconut
2 drops of vanilla essence

Method:

- Drain the peaches and arrange them in a dish.
- Separate the egg whites and yolks. Whisk the whites. Set aside the yolks.
- Heat the milk in a pan.
- Beat the egg yolks and sugar for 5 minutes. Pour into the warm milk, stirring continuously until the custard thickens. Remove from the heat and leave to cool.
- When cool, add the whisked egg whites and a few drops of vanilla essence.
- Pour the custard over the peaches and refrigerate until serving.

Baked bananas, Catalan-style

YOLK & ALMOND "TURRÓN"

Serves: 6
Difficulty: medium
Required time: 45 minutes (plus resting time – approx. 1 day)

Ingredients:

For 1 kg of "turrón"

500 g ground raw almonds
500 g sugar
half a glass of water
3 egg yolks
100 g condensed milk or cream
vanilla essence or lemon juice

Sugared yolk:

2 egg yolks
sugar (the same weight as the yolks)
fresh fruit for garnish
icing sugar

Method:

- Make a caramel syrup by boiling the sugar and water.
- Put the finely-ground almonds in a bowl. Add the caramel and stir well.
- Add the yolks one by one. Mix well.
- Add the condensed milk or cream.
- Stir well and add a few drops of vanilla essence or lemon juice.
- Line a rectangular mould with aluminium foil. Fill with the "turrón" mixture.
- Leave in a cool place for about 24 hours.
- Unmould. Remove the aluminium foil and return the "turrón" to the mould.
- Cover with the sugared yolk* and sprinkle with icing sugar.
- Caramelise topping by applying a special hot rod.
- Serve accompanied with slices of fresh fruit, such as kiwis, strawberries, pears, pineapple, etc.

***Sugared yolk:**

- Beat the egg yolks and sugar well.
- Heat in a saucepan, stirring continuously with a wooden spatula/spoon.
- When the mixture starts to thicken and to stick to the spatula/spoon, remove pan from heat.
- Keep on stirring and return to the heat.
- Before it reaches boiling point, remove from heat again and beat well.
- Turn onto a tray and leave to cool.
- Use when cold.

Yolk & almond "turrón"

ALPHABETICAL INDEX OF RECIPES